ESETOMES is the brand name for titles written by Eric Otis Simmons. It is derived from, **E**ric **S**immons **E**nterprises, Inc., followed by the word **TOMES** (books in a work of several volumes).

The "Self Publisher's Toolkit" provides information on how to self publish a book, the steps typically involved, and some of the self publishing resources and "platforms" available. The reader is also provided information on how to engage a specific market segment, in this case, Libraries, with their self published work.

There is no guaranty made that self publishing of any book or other written or spoken language publication will generate any income, nor is there a guaranty of results. The same applies to the marketing of a self published book to a segment such as Libraries. In addition to the lack of any guaranty, express, or implied, there is also no express or implied warranty. Purchaser or any third party that receives this publication from a purchaser hereby acknowledges and agrees that the Author makes no representation or warranty, express or implied, at law or in equity, in any respect to any matter relating to the contents of this publication including, without limitation, any strategy, course of action, or other undertaking.

The Purchaser hereby waives any and all claims that may arise as a result of any actions or other activities or lack of same by the Purchaser or any third party that may or may not have resulted from the content contained within this Publication. Purchaser agrees to indemnify and defend the Author, the Author's representatives, heirs, assigns, or designees against any and all claims by the Purchaser or any third party.

Self Publishers Toolkit

Copyright © 2020 by Eric Simmons Enterprises, Inc.

All rights are reserved. No part of this book may be reproduced or transmitted in any form or by any means without written permission from the Author.

ISBN 9780578723938

Dedication

This book is dedicated to my mother, Wiletta. She touched many lives, especially mine, with her willingness to share information and knowledge with others, especially when she felt it would be helpful and beneficial.

Acknowledgments

My thanks to my wife, Cynthia, for supporting me in this writing endeavor. My appreciation also to the companies that have developed "platforms," which enable us to share our self published works with others. Lastly, thank you to the hundreds of Librarians around the world for their vote of confidence in my written works.

About the Author

Without any prior book writing experience or knowledge of the publishing industry, on March 7, 2017, Eric Otis Simmons released his self published Memoir, "**Not Far From The Tree.**" From January 2019, when Simmons began tracking the book's Amazon "**Best Seller**" sales results, through the date of this publication, the title had appeared on the list 24 times.

Eric, a Certified Webmaster, is the CEO/Founder of ESE, Inc., a website development firm. His company specializes in creating custom websites for Authors, Poets, compensation eligible College Athletes, High School Athletes, and others seeking to present their "Personal Brand" on the Internet for marketing, brand establishment, athletic recruitment, or similar purposes. His written works are copyrighted under the brand name of ESETOMES, which stands for ESE, Inc. plus the word TOMES (books in a work of several volumes). In addition to this book and his Memoir, his other self published titles, in order of publication are, **"#HTSP - How to Self-Publish**," "**ESETOMES Box Set**," an eBook compilation of his first two books and "**Getting Your Book Into Libraries**." At the time of this publication, and since January 2019, his titles, combined, had made 37 appearances on Amazon's "Best Seller" list and since January 2018, the books had been ranked in the "Top 1%"

About the Author

in worldwide sales 80 times and the "Top 10%," 501 times. His article, **"How To Get Your Book Into Libraries,"** became the top Google search result, excluding Ads, out of over 2 billion results on the subject of "getting your book into libraries." Simmons and his wife reside in metro Atlanta, and they have three adult children.

ESETOMES Books
Website - www.eseinc1.com/esetomes-books
Facebook - www.facebook.com/esimmonsauthor
Twitter – www.twitter.com/esimmonsauthor

ESE, Inc.
Website - www.eseinc1.com
Facebook - www.facebook.com/ESE-Inc-1431136640304095/?ref=br_rs

Contents

Dedication	i
Acknowledgments	ii
About the Author	iii
Contents	v
Publisher versus Self Publishing	vi
Chapter 1 - Self Publishing in the 2020s	1
Market Outlook	1
The ABCs of Self Publishing	9
A – Write Your Book	10
B - Package Your Book	27
C - Channelize and Market Your Book	45
Chapter 2 - Marketing Your Book	59
Chapter 3 - Setting Up Your Book Business	66
Chapter 4 - Managing Your Book Business	69
Chapter 5 – Marketing Your Book to Libraries	75
Why Libraries?	75
Chapter 6 - Getting Started Marketing to Libraries	87
Chapter 7 - Building Your "Library Contacts Database"	95
Chapter 8 - Creating a "Mail Merge" Document	101
Chapter 9 – Tactics	104
Chapter 10 – Methodology Summary	115
References	117

Publisher versus Self Publishing

For many, the decision to self publish a book may be intuitive and come quickly, whereas, for others, validation may be needed as to whether one should go through a publisher or self publish. I fell into the latter category, even though I was pretty sure I wanted to self publish my first book. To validate the direction I felt I would be heading in, I decided to invest some time doing Google research to gain a better understanding of the differences between going through a publisher and taking the self publishing route. I came across an article entitled, "Pros And Cons Of Traditional Publishing vs Self-Publishing," which proved quite beneficial. The piece was written by Joanna Penn, a best-selling Author who had transitioned from the traditional Publisher route to self publishing. After reviewing Penn's information, I created a T-Chart with Publisher on the left side and Self Publish on the right. Underneath each heading, I listed the pros and cons. As a "visual learner," I felt seeing information in this format would help me in deciding between the two alternatives.

When I concluded my research, I was able to confirm "Self Publishing" would be the best route for me because the "Pros" outweighed the "Cons," in my view. Following is a synopsis of my notes from my research:

Decision - Publisher or Self Publish

Publisher

Pros
- Prestige
- Sales to Bookstores

Cons
- Slow Process (1-2 Years to Launch)
- Royalties 7%-25% (generously)
- Agents/Contracts
- May be Complex

Self Publish

Pros
- Control and Faster Time to Market
- Higher Royalties
  - Mine: 16%-70% (Kindle)
- Rights Retention
- Pick who you sell to/through

Cons
- Everything is On You
- Stigma Due to Poor Works
- May Need Editor/Designer

Copyright © 2020 ESE, Inc.

Publisher

Pros

- Prestige
- Distribution to bookstores via Sales Representatives
- An Advance (i.e., upfront money) to the Author

    Note: Per Penn, "…the advance is against royalties, which are usually 7-25% of the net book price. Royalties can be 10% on average. So, if you get an advance of $10,000, you then have to earn more than $10,000 out of your royalty rate on your book sales before you get any more money."

Cons

- Slow process. Could take 1-2.5 years before your book launch
- Royalties of 7-25% with the latter being generous. Hard to predict cash flow
- Involves contracts and could be complex
- May need an Agent

Self Publish

Pros

- Total "**creative control**" over content and design
- Faster time to market!
- Higher Royalties.
  Note: Amazon Kindle can be up to 70%!
- Retain your rights to your book
- Pick and choose who to sell your book to and through

Cons

- Virtually, everything is on you
- You may need to find:
  - A proofreader/editor
  - Cover Designer

- The "Stigma" around Self Publishers (i.e., are you legit)
    - A lot of poorly written self published books
- May be challenging to get into bookstores
- Might be hard to get noticed for literary awards

Chapter 1
Self Publishing in the 2020s

Market Outlook

In researching the future of self publishing for this book, current indicators are, growth is expected for the industry in 2020 and beyond. In October 2019, Bowker, the exclusive U.S. agent for issuing International Standard Book Numbers (ISBNs), released findings from a study its affiliate ProQuest had conducted about the self publishing industry. ProQuest's data revealed, "... self publishing grew at a rate of 40 percent in 2018 – and shows no signs of slowing down." In the release, Beat Barblan, Vice President of Publishing and Data Services at Bowker and chairman of the board of the International ISBN Agency, is quoted as saying, "The self publishing landscape continues to improve, creating more and more opportunities for authors to manage their own path through the process." Barblan also went on to say, "As more authors take advantage of the abundant tools now available to publish, distribute and market their own books, we expect that self publishing will continue to grow at a steady pace."

In a Forbes.com October 2019 article, "While $26 Billion Publishing Industry Is Flat, This Vertical Segment Is Exploding.

Leverage These Insights To Ride The Wave," Bernhard Schroeder wrote, "An annual report from the Association of American Publishers indicated that the U.S. book publishing industry generated an estimated $26.23 billion in net revenue for 2017, representing 2.72 billion books. While this revenue is fairly flat, year over year, self publishing is rapidly rising with e-books, print on demand, and audiobooks bringing in billions of U.S. dollars in revenue each year."

Self Publishing Jargon

To be able to "walk the walk" in the book world, you'll find it helpful to be able to "talk the talk." Familiarizing yourself with some of the "Lingo" used in the book "publishing" world will not only help boost your confidence when speaking with customers, fellow authors, and others; it can help enhance your credibility as well.

Due to my unfamiliarity with some of the terms used in the book publishing industry, early on in my self publishing career, I came close to what would have been an extremely embarrassing moment. I had emailed a Library some information about my first book, and I received a response back informing me the book had been sent over to the Library's Collections Department for review. I became upset because I had no delinquent accounts with anyone and couldn't imagine why a Collection Agency would be involved. Moments before I was about to fire off a blistering email to the Librarian who had emailed me, I decided to do a Google search to see if the word Collection meant something different in the Library world. It turns out the term refers to the books and other materials in a Library. Imagine how embarrassing it would have been if I had sent the email. I would have lost all credibility with the Library for not knowing what is perhaps their most widely used term. The following are a few terms used in the book publishing industry that I feel you should know so that you might avoid a potentially embarrassing moment like mine.

Independent Author, Indie, Indie Author, Self Publisher

In the book industry, you'll hear terms such as Independent Author, Indie, Indie Author, and Self Publisher to describe you and me.

Title

Oxford Dictionary defines title as the name of a book, composition, or other artistic work.

Genre

Merriam-Webster defines genre as "a category of artistic, musical, or literary composition characterized by a particular style, form, or content."

Understanding information about your book's genre, such as the category's annual sales, expected market opportunities, and titles your manuscript will be competing against, will help you in developing a marketing strategy for your book.

Per Wikipedia, genres fall into two categories, Fiction and Non-Fiction, and according to Query*Tracker,* Young Adult is the most popular Fiction genre while Memoirs top their list as the most popular Non-Fiction genre.

Genres

10 Most Popular Fiction	10 Most Popular Non-Fiction
1 Young Adult	1 Memoirs
2 Fantasy	2 Self-Help
3 Children's	3 Narrative
4 Literary Fiction	4 Religion/Spirituality
5 Science Fiction	5 Biography
6 Thrillers/Suspense	6 Cultural/Social Issues
7 Middle Grade	7 Business/Finance
8 Romance	8 History
9 Picture Books	9 General Non-Fiction
10 Historical	10 Health/Fitness

Source: Query*Tracker*

As to revenue by genre, according to a January 31, 2014 article, on the Richest.com website, by Thomas Stewart entitled, "**Which 5 Book Genres Make The Most Money?**," the "Top 5" earning genres were:

1. Romance/Erotica - $1.44 billion
2. Crime/Mystery - $728.2 million
3. Religious/Inspirational - $720 million
4. Science Fiction/Fantasy - $590.2 million
5. Horror - $79.6 million

I created the following chart so that you can see what the above $3.6 billion in revenue generated by the "Top 5" looks like percentage-wise.

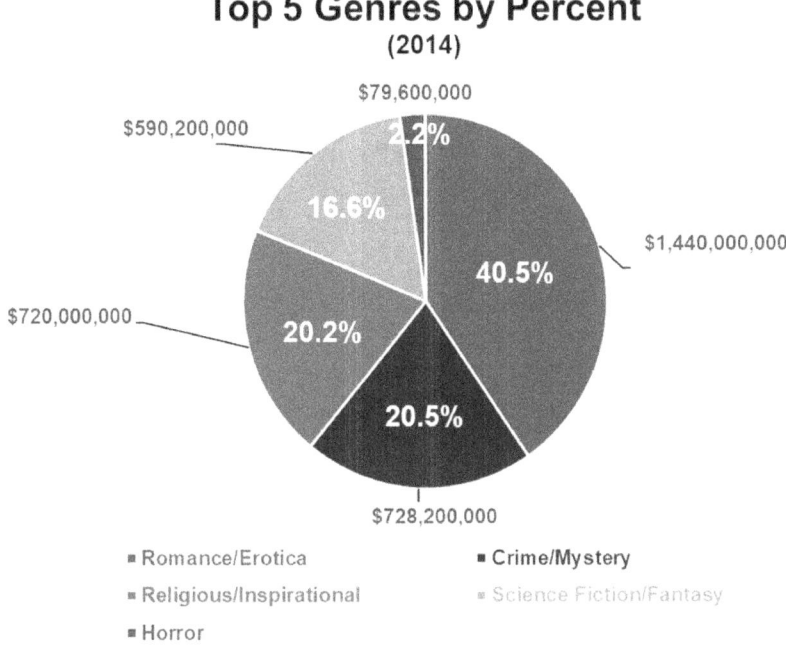

International Standard Book Number (ISBN)

Per SEG Wiki, an International Standard Book Number or ISBN is a unique numeric commercial book identifier. An ISBN is assigned to each edition and variation (except reprintings) of a book.

You will have an important decision to make regarding ISBNs. It will be whether you will want to use a free ISBN provided by many of the companies that offer printing and distributing services for your book or use an ISBN that you purchase, which is often referred to as a "Universal ISBN." The difference is significant. A free ISBN will show the company that provided it to you as the "Publisher of Record," which is defined as the entity in whose name the book's ISBN is registered. When you purchase an ISBN, however, you are recognized as the entity to which the book's ISBN is recorded, and the same applies if you use your company's name.

Simply put, whose name do you want to have shown on your book as the publisher? The free ISBN provider or yours? As a word of caution, if you find a "low priced" ISBN, do read the fine print because the provider may list themselves as the "Publisher of Record." How can this be, you ask? Well, some less than forthcoming companies, I feel, won't expect you to read the fine print. As a rule of thumb, and from pricing I've seen, a "Universal ISBN" will typically cost in the eighty dollar range and up, and have in the provider's written information, some type of acknowledgment of you, or your company, as the "Publisher of Record."

The free versus fee ISBN debate yields over six hundred million search results, so it just goes to show, there are a lot of opinions on the matter. Currently, I have a "Universal ISBN" for each of my paperback titles, and I use free ISBNs for my eBooks. To date, none of the purchasers of my paperback or eBooks have informed me my use of multiple ISBNs (i.e., free of "Universal) has been problematic.

Sites with Book Industry Terminology

Should you come across book publishing industry terms that you are unfamiliar with, several sites that offer definitions are:

- Nathan Bransford, "Book publishing glossary" – https://blog.nathanbransford.com/book-publishing-glossary

- Bookjobs.com "Commonly Used Terms" – http://www.bookjobs.com/commonly-used-terms

The ABCs of Self Publishing

At its core, self publishing can be broken down into three fundamental areas that I will refer to as the ABCs of Self Publishing. Each of these areas has underlying components that I will describe in more detail.

A - Write Your Book
B - Package Your Book
C - Channelize and Market Your Book

A → Write Your Book

B → Package Your Book

C → Channelize and Market Your Book

A – Write Your Book

This area concerns itself with the task of writing one's manuscript. The first step is to get started, which, for many, is easier said than done, it seems.

According to a 2002 survey conducted by The New York Times, "81% of Americans feel they have a book in them - and that they should write it." Fast forward to April 24, 2020, when Statista.com reported that in 2019, there were over 45.8 thousand writers and authors working in the United States. I'm assuming self published authors were included in the total because they are mentioned in the same paragraph. So, of the three hundred twenty-eight (328) million people living in America in 2019, per the U.S. Census Bureau, less that one percent (0.014%) of the U.S. population was engaged in writing books. What happened to the other 80% that felt they should write a book? My guess is they had trouble getting started writing their manuscript, which was the problem I experienced with my first book.

As background, from 2005 through 2017, I started and stopped writing my manuscript a total of 12 times. I also re-titled my first book, seven (7) times. Finally, on September 25, 2016, I decided on a title and began writing my book. Why was I having such a hard time getting started? Was it procrastination? If so, why was I procrastinating? After having spent most of my career in sales with some of America's largest companies, I was comfortable with writing emails, memos, and proposals. Still, for some reason, I couldn't get started writing my book. My excuses tended to be, "I'm too busy right now," or "I'll get around to it later."

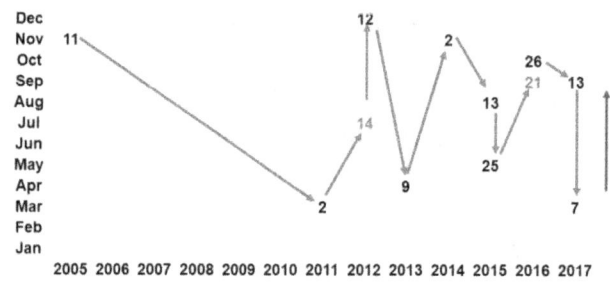

If you've found yourself having trouble getting started writing your book, you're not alone. There are a lot of reasons why people probably procrastinate about writing their first book. Amongst them could be: fear of rejection, concern as to whether people will like the book, a lack of confidence in one's writing skills, and others. It wasn't until I took a hard look at why I wanted to write a book in the first place, that I was able to break the grip procrastination had on me.

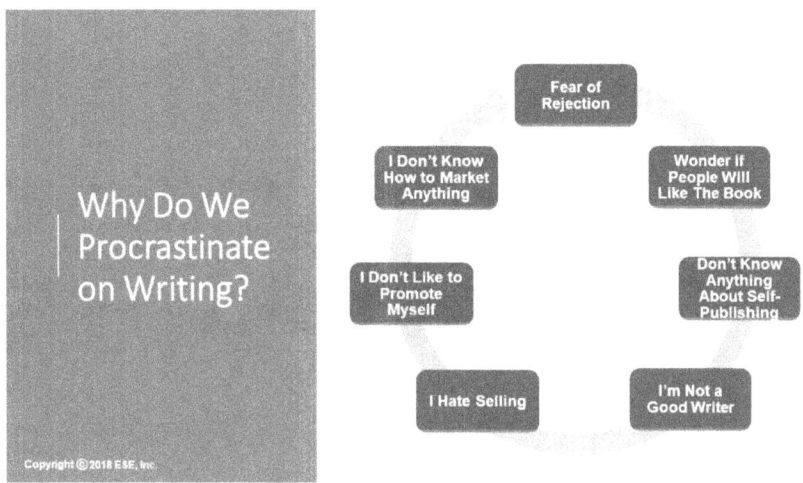

Identify Your Purpose for Writing

I was able to overcome my procrastination by documenting why I had decided to write a book in the first place. I refer to this decision point as my "Leap of Faith" moment. There were three reasons why I wanted to write a book. The first was, I wanted to provide a "leave behind" for my children. Doing so would require me to open up to them and share information about myself and my life that they may not have known. Second, I sought to document our family tree and provide the backgrounds and numerous accomplishments of our forebearers so that my children could take pride in and feel good about their heritage. Third, through the sharing of my life experiences and successes, I wanted to inspire youth, particularly African American ones, who, like me, may have come from single-parent backgrounds.

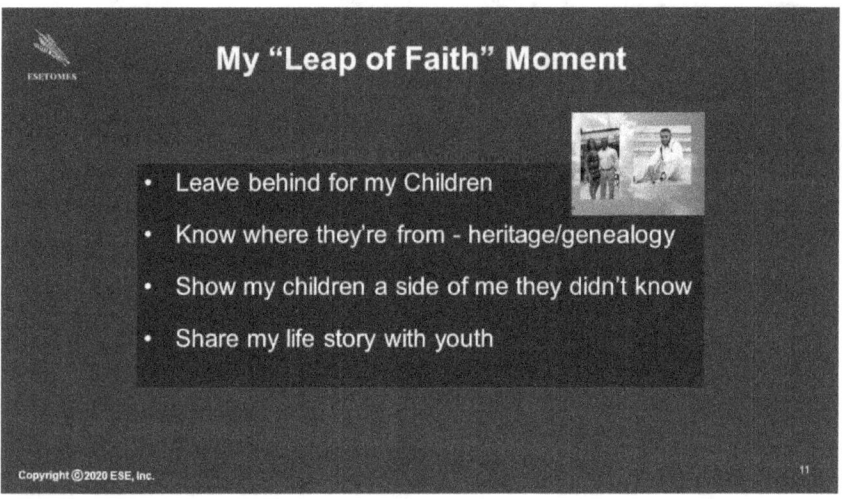

With my "purpose for writing," laid out before me, I now had the motivation and courage to proceed with penning my book. Going forward, whenever I found myself faced with "writing procrastination," I would refer back to my purpose. So, if you're stuck in getting started writing your book, step back and think about what it was that made you want to write in the first place.

Writing Your Book

You will find writing your first book to be both challenging yet immensely rewarding. It will require planning, preparation, organization, patience, creativity, and stick-to-itiveness on your part. You will sweat the smallest of details associated with your book as you strive to produce a quality piece of work for readers to enjoy.

Goal Setting

Writing a book is a project, and as a result, it will require goal setting on your part to achieve your objectives of self publishing your book and getting it to market. Writing down your goals, if you haven't done so already, will give you something to work towards and help keep you focused on your objective. Your goals will help serve as a roadmap to guide you along your writing journey. I'll use my goals for the "Self Publisher's Toolkit" to serve as an example. They were 1). Provide you with a helpful "resource" aimed at reducing your learning curve and simplifying the self publishing process so that you can get your book to market sooner. 2). Give you a "tool" that you can refer back to during the various stages of your book writing and sales channel development. 3).

Share my Library tactics and methodology with you so that you will have a market, in addition to the retail sector, that you can begin pursuing right away.

Planning, Preparation, and Organization

When you begin your book writing process, it is essential to get organized. I suggest writing down your thoughts about what you plan to cover in your book, in an outline format. I tend to use Microsoft Word for this process. Next, jot down your main points, or topics, in bullet points, or similar. These bulleted items become your Chapters, and information underneath each bullet becomes content within the Chapters. Having your outline in a Word document will allow you to move things around until they make sense to you from an organization standpoint. When you complete portions of your book, highlight the completed section in your outline. This "checking off" process can help serve as a "reward," so to speak, as it will allow you to see the progress you are making with your book.

Font Selection

For my first self published book, I spent an excessive amount of time, I feel, researching the type of font to use for a book. I came to learn; there are "preferred" fonts for the interior of a book, which are more acceptable, literary-wise, and to readers than others for particular genres. To illustrate, in an InDesignSkills article, "Best Fonts for Books: The Only 5 Fonts You'll Ever Need," the site suggests:

1. For Literary Fiction: Baskerville
2. For Romantic Fiction: Sabon
3. For Thrillers and Airport Page-Turners: Garamond
4. For Academic Non-Fiction: Caslon
5. For General Interest: Utopia

While the above list is just one opinion, I suggest you try to determine the interior and exterior fonts used by successful Authors, such as those of best-selling books, in your genre. If you can't decide which font they are using, choose from the top one or two found when you do a Google search on fonts for your particular genre. It's best to stay status quo with fonts that are widely used in your book's category, I feel. If you're using Microsoft Word to create your book, and the font you've decided on isn't available, you can download fonts from the Internet. Some are free, and some are for a fee.

In terms of choosing a font for your book's front and back cover, if you were to Google, "What's the best font for a book cover?" you would get nearly 8 million search results. As a result, I recommend using a graphics designer experienced in creating book covers for your genre. An experienced designer should be familiar with suitable fonts for your book's category. I have used freelancers on Fiverr.com, a global online marketplace offering tasks and freelance services, for my book covers. On Fiverr's site, you will be able to search for freelancers providing a variety of services, including book cover design. When you search for "book cover," as an example, you will find nearly seven thousand (7,000) services available. You will be able to review cover designs, see the rating designers have received for their work, set your price range for a cover, and more. Should you want to explore other companies that offer freelance services, Owler.com lists Fiverr's top ten competitors at www.owler.com/company/fiverr.

A – Write Your Book   Chapter 1

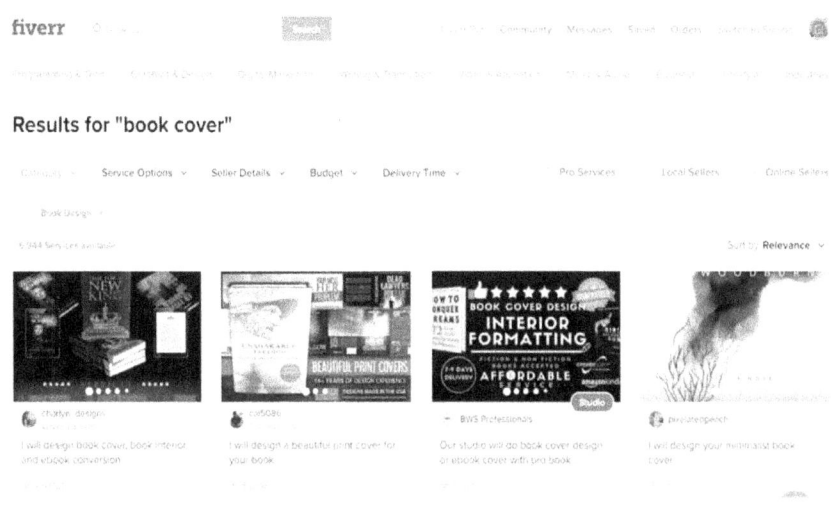

Ultimately, the font(s) you choose for the interior and exterior of your book is entirely up to you. That's one of the beauties of self publishing. The end decision is yours. When it doubt, though, it's best to go with generally accepted book industry practices.

Setting Aside Time to Write

As with any project, having a schedule in place can help keep you on track. Hence, I would encourage you to set aside time or an amount of time each day that you will spend writing your book. For my first title, I established an amount of time of at least 4 hours a day. No matter what time I started my writing, I would try to write for 4 hours and take a break whenever I felt I needed one. While you may not always meet your daily writing goals, timewise, that's okay because there will be times when you exceed your goal. When this happens, you'll be in what I refer to as a "writing zone." That is, your words on paper will start flowing so well, you won't want to stop writing. The whole idea around scheduling is to try to build some structure and discipline around your writing so that you can ultimately complete your book.

Tools to Help You Write

Speech to Text Software

When I sat down to write my first book, it didn't take me long to realize I was going nowhere fast. My issue was I had never learned how to type! As you might imagine, being a "hunt and peck," typist is not a good thing, productivity-wise, when you are trying to write a book. Fortunately, I had purchased some speech to text software, a few years earlier, in anticipation of me writing a book, so I dusted it off and put it to use. The product was Dragon NaturallySpeaking, developed by Nuance Communications. Today, the software is called Dragon Professional. I was also able to find the headset I had purchased to use with the software.

I was surprised and pleased by how easy it was for me to train the Dragon software to recognize my voice once I had installed the application on my computer. The software also quickly "learned" my writing style after it had analyzed previous emails and Word documents I had written. The incorporation of speech to text technology caused my book writing productivity to go through the roof! I was able to complete large sections of my manuscript quickly and efficiently. If you haven't thought about using speech to text technology, for your book, I suggest you give it a try.

Microsoft Office Dictation

For my second self published book, I gave Microsoft Office Dictation a try, since it was a part of my Microsoft 365 subscription. I used the application to dictate the entire book, and while I found it to be pretty easy to use, it wasn't quite as intuitive as Nuance's product, I felt. If you have a Microsoft subscription and don't want to pay for a speech to text software program like Dragon Professional, I believe you'll find Office Dictation to be a viable alternative.

Grammarly

Grammarly is the tool I use for grammar, spell checking, and sentence structure assistance. For my first book, I paid monthly for the product, but became so impressed with it; I purchased an annual license. Now, in addition to using the product for book writing help, I use it for all of my correspondence. I view Grammarly as my first line of defense for "editing," and I believe it helps me keep my overall self publishing costs down. I also feel it complements services provided by a professional proofreader or editor as well. Lastly, the Alliance for Independent Authors (ALLI), which I'll talk about in section B – Package Your Book, also recommends Grammarly.

Strategies for Your Book

Set a Target Number of Pages

When I was working on my Memoir, it became painfully clear the book could get quite large. As a result, I decided to try to keep the manuscript to around two hundred (200) pages. Page count management turned out to be a wise decision on my part because up until the time I submitted my book for printing, I was unaware print cost goes up at certain page count levels. Using Amazon's Kindle Direct Publishing (KDP) group's print book calculator, which you can download for free, the print cost for my Memoir at two hundred (200) pages was $3.25. At two hundred one (201) pages, the price increased to $3.27. My paperback ended up being two hundred thirty pages, and the print cost was $3.61. So as you can see, page count affects your print cost, which is something you will want to take into account when determining your book's selling price, a topic I will discuss in section C.

My decision to set a "targeted number of pages" for my book had an added benefit. It became a "discipline check," so to speak, in that it caused me to put more thought into what needed to be in the book and what didn't. Subsequently, I ended up removing close to one hundred pages of what I thought was extraneous information. If you anticipate you are going to have a large number of pages and depending on your genre, you might want to consider a series, a method that seems to have worked well for some self published authors.

Keep Writing When You "Get on a Roll"

Some days you will get on a roll, and you will want to keep writing. Continue to do so, even if what you are writing seems out of place at the time. I take my "displaced" information and put it at the end of the book on a page or pages that I call a "placeholder." Interestingly, I've found that about seventy percent (70%) of the material in my "placeholder" ended up in my book. It turns out the information was needed, after all, just somewhere else.

Proofread Your Work Regularly

While proofreading your work may be common sense, it can't be overstated. You will be surprised at things you will catch and that you can improve upon in your book by merely taking the time to proofread your work. Also, have your title proofread and edited by someone if necessary. The more eyes on your work, before you put it out into the marketplace, the better.

Dealing with Writer's Block

Writer's block is such a common occurrence amongst authors that when Googled, you'll get over forty-five million search results! My theory about writer's block is, when one is writing a book, their concentration level is so high, and they are so focused, that over time they begin to tire and wear down a bit. When this happens, it creates writer's block.

Per Wikipedia, a study of 2500 writers was undertaken to find out about techniques that writers were using to overcome writer's block. The research discovered a range of solutions from altering the time of day to write, to set deadlines to lowering expectations and using mindfulness meditation. Research has also shown that it is highly effective if one breaks their work into pieces rather than trying to do all of their writing in one sitting, to produce good quality work.

With *Not Far From The Tree*, I experienced writer's block to the extent I had to get away from writing for two weeks. Some of the things I believe you and I can do to address writer's block is to take frequent breaks, go for a walk, watch some TV, and reward ourselves when we complete a milestone with our book. The key, perhaps, is to engage in another type of activity so we can "break the monotony" and get out of our funk. Remembering our "purpose for writing" should also help get us back on track.

So, when you hit the wall and experience writer's block, know you're not alone, and it probably won't last forever. Once your battery is recharged, you'll be back on your way to writing.

Use of Third-Party Material

If you use material from someone else, such as photos, articles, etc., be sure to denote the originator someplace in your book, such as the "References" section. Just because the material is in the "Public Domain," such as the Internet, doesn't necessarily mean it isn't copyright protected.

When I identify photos or images on the Worldwide Web that I would like to use, before I do so, I choose "Settings" under the Google search bar and select "Advanced search," which, when clicked, takes me to a screen named "Advanced Image Search." Near the bottom of the screen, there is a "usage rights" line item that has "not filtered by license" as the default value of a drop-down menu. I click on the drop-down arrow, and from the menu choices, I select "free to use, share or modify, even commercially." This way, I will receive "hits" on items where the originator has granted use. There have also been times when I have reached out directly to the originator of a photo or image via phone or email to request permission to use their work. If I don't get a return call or email response, I make a note of such. I do so in the event I'm asked by the owner to remove the content. At a minimum, I will be able to let the owner know the date I had attempted to contact him/her for permission. It is always better to reach out, if you are unsure about the use of material, rather than run the risk of copyright infringement.

B – Package Your Book

As with any construction or "building" project, a solid foundation is needed to support the structure. You also need a budget to pay for things such as labor and materials. Foundation setting and budgeting also apply to your self published book. Educating yourself on self publishing helps you build a foundation as to how to proceed in the marketplace. Once your project has been completed, you will need to incorporate "packaging," which Entreprenuer.com defines as, "The wrapping material around a consumer item that serves to contain, identify, describe, protect, display, promote and otherwise make the product marketable and keep it clean." In this section, I will discuss some of the self publishing resources available to you, go over budgeting for your book, and share companies that you can work with to help you "package" your title. To me, packaging involves all of the steps and resources outside of your writing that need to take place to get your book ready for sale.

Self Publishing Resources

To begin laying a solid foundation for your book, you will need resources such as *The Self Publisher's Toolkit*. Some additional resources available to you are:

- Self Publishing Advice from the Alliance of Independent Authors - https://selfpublishingadvice.org/
    - This site is made available by the Alliance of Independent Authors (ALLi) and is one of my favorite resources. ALLi is a non-profit professional association for authors who self publish. You can search on Alli's site for information on ISBNs, for example, and also find interesting articles such as "Book Production: 12 Avoidable Rookie Errors" by Debbie Young.

- The Creative Penn website - https://www.thecreativepenn.com
    - This website is filled with helpful information, a lot of which is free.

- The Indie View - http://www.theindieview.com

- This site has a section called "The Indie Reviewers List," which is where you can find a list of Independent Authors who have indicated their willingness to review fellow Indie Authors' books for "Free." The Authors also list the genres they review.

Before you start doing cartwheels about the "Free" review, let me share with you my experience. For my first book, I contacted 16 reviewers, and I heard back from three. Two told me they were going to place me in their queue for a review, and I never heard back from them. The third, a self publisher based in Athens, Greece, accommodated me. He had written over twenty books at the time, and when he emailed me to make me aware he would review my book, he confirmed it would be for free. All he asked for in return was for me to review a book he had just finished. Although I had no previous experience reviewing books, I took advantage of the opportunity to learn about that side of the business. After reading my book, the reviewer rated it 5-stars and posted his review on Amazon.com and Goodreads. He also published his assessment on his website for his European followers. So, I believe I got "lucky" with my reviewer.

Keep in mind, book reviews by entities such as Publishers Weekly and Library Journal tend to carry more weight with many readers and Librarians than say, those from who you may or may not know. If you are looking for a "Free" book review, however, The Indie View and Goodreads are several sources, provided you can find an available reviewer.

- Authors' Websites
  - Visiting various Authors' websites will give you ideas for your future site, and you'll get to see the variety of ways in which Authors are marketing their books and themselves.

- Authors' Biographies
  - Reviewing the biographies of other Authors will help you formulate ideas for your own.

Self Publishing Resources   Chapter 1

More about the author

› Visit Amazon's Eric O Simmons Page

Biography
Biography

Eric Simmons, a graduate of Auburn University and former DI athlete (basketball), spent
of Sales/Sales Management positions with Fortune 500 employers IBM, AT&T, GE, MCI a
business travels, he closed sales of $500,000 (Paris), $1 million (Brussels), and $25 millic
Inc., a Consulting firm. His motivational Memoir, "Not Far From The Tree" is his first publ

+ Follow

- Articles About Indie Authors
    - Reading articles about and by Indie Authors who have had success will keep you motivated and inspired. One story that I enjoyed was an Entreprenuer.com piece by Rob Dircks entitled, "5 Things This Self-Published Author Did to Sell Over 20,000 Books With Almost No Money." The article is about Rob's first self published book, and he highlights five things he did to help drive the book's success. While Rob's achievement with his first book is more of an "outlier," I feel it illustrates that with a good book, a solid marketing plan, and determination, one can achieve self publishing success.

Establish a Budget For Your Book

If you haven't done so already, I encourage you to establish a budget for your book. The reason being, the costs associated with self publishing can add up quickly if you're not careful. With my first title, and not knowing the costs involved with self publishing a book, I established a budget of five hundred dollars ($500) for the project. Since I was using personal funds, this amount was the maximum I was willing to spend at the time. I also felt having an "investment" target amount in mind would help me avoid "cost overruns." Unfortunately, I didn't use a spreadsheet or financial accounting tool to track my expenditures. Instead, I was, more or less, keeping up with my cash "outflows" mentally. In January 2018, I created a spreadsheet to analyze how much I had spent on self publishing my first book. I ended up being one hundred eighty-one dollars and eighty-four cents ($181.84) over budget for the project.

Establish a Budget For Your Book — Chapter 1

Budgeting

How Much Did I Spend?

Description	Monthly/OneTime	Total
Book Giveaways	$299.84	$299.84
Universal ISBN	$99.00	$99.00
Facebook Ad	$50.00	$50.00
Ingram	$49.00	$49.00
Book Show	$40.00	$40.00
Library of Congress Filing	$35.00	$35.00
Business Cards/Bookmarks	$25.00	$25.00
Wix Website	$14.00	$84.00
Subtotal		$681.84
Less Universal ISBN		($99.00)
Less Library of Congress Filing		($35.00)
Total		$547.84
Cut Book Giveaways in Half		($149.92)
Revised Total		$397.92

[1] $3.61 − $3.59 − $0.28 − $3.00 = **$10.48**

KDP Expanded Distribution re: ISBN. The paperback can have an ISBN you bought or one assigned by KDP. Your book's ISBN must not have been submitted for distribution through another service.

Copyright © 2020 ESC, Inc.

For my second book, *#HTSP – How to Self-Publish*, I was able to set a more realistic budget, based on my experience with my first book. I was able to set a slightly lower budget the second time around because I now realized book giveaways had cost me dearly with my Memoir. It turned out; giveaways represented nearly half of my inaugural book's expense. It became apparent to me if I were to give away just a few books, or none at all, the second time around, I could cut my expenses nearly in half! This time, I used a spreadsheet to track my financial outlays for *#HTSP*, as I call it, as they were occurring. After I reviewed the book's expenses associated with "getting it out of the door," at the end of the year, I ended up coming in at right around budget!

Establish a Budget For Your Book   Chapter 1

My #HTSP - How to Self-Publish Budget

Description	Quantity	Estimated Budget
Universal ISBN	1	$99.00
Ingram	1	$49.00
Graphic Design	1	$50.00
Advertising	2	$40.00
Proof and Shipping (CreateSpace, Ingram, Barnes & Noble)	3	$30.00
Initial Inventory	2	$12.00
Other (Proofs, etc.)	1	$20.00
Total		$300.00

My rationale for upfront budgeting and trying to keep my book "start-up costs" low is I'm trying to achieve profitability within three (3) years for each of my books following their release. Setting a profitability timeline for your book is something I would strongly encourage you to do.

Book Distributors

Print Books - Paperback/Hard Copy

After you've completed your writing, editing, review, and cover selection process for your book, you will need to decide on who you want to have print and distribute it, if you haven't done so already. Many businesses offer book printing and distribution services for Indie Authors. In, "The 12 BEST Self-Publishing Companies of 2020," Reedsy.com listed those they felt were tops. The article describes self publishing companies as "service providers" and not publishers, who fall into three categories:

- Book Retailers (such as Amazon)
- Aggregators (who allow you to distribute to a bunch of book retailers all at once)
- Print on Demand (POD) Distributors (full-suite self-publishing companies that include print-on-demand services on top of distribution options)

In this section, I'll discuss the companies I'm currently using, which happen to be ten of the ones on Reedsy's list, and I'll use the terms "provider" and "service provider" interchangeably to describe the group unless further clarification is necessary.

The provider selection process may seem daunting at first, but there are resources available to help you narrow down your selections. In addition to Reedsy's listing, ALLi has developed an aid called, "The Best Self-Publishing Services–and the Worst–Rated." In addition to service providers, the tool lists over one hundred companies that offer a variety of services ranging from editing to transcription to publishing and more. All of the companies in the "database" have a color-coded rating, based on ALLi's assessment of multiple criteria. These include pricing and value, quality of service, contract terms and rights, transparency, accountability, and customer satisfaction. Green denotes companies whose services have been vetted by ALLi and meet the organization's Code of Standards. Blue indicates companies that have been observed to behave ethically and professionally, with pricing and value in line with industry norms. There is a color code that denotes companies that have received mixed reviews, one for those to be cautious about, and red is used to highlight companies that have received consistent complaints and, in some cases, have been subject to legal action.

Partnership between Aliant University and **Author Solutions**			
Amazon (CreateSpace)	🔗	★ Partner Member	
Read our comparison of **Ingram Spark vs. CreateSpace**, and learn how you can **use both services** to leverage the strengths of each.			
Amazon (KDP)	🔗	★ Partner Member	
Read our comparison of publishing platforms in **Amazon vs. Apple**			
America Star Books		⚠ Watchdog Advisory	Legal, Value, Communication, Service, Transparency, Marketing, Quality
Formerly PublishAmerica, a vanity press with a staggering number of **complaints**			
Amnet Systems	🔗	★ Partner Member	
Amolibros	🔗	★ Partner Member	
Anthemion Software	🔗	★ Partner Member	
Apple (iBooks)	🔗	✓ Recommended	
Read our comparison of publishing platforms in **Amazon vs. Apple**			
Archway Publishing		⚠ Watchdog Advisory	Legal, Value, Communication, Service, Transparency, Marketing, Quality

I used Alli's best and worst self publishers list to identify prospective paperback service providers for my first book. By most accounts, the top-rated company, at the time, was CreateSpace, a business unit of Amazon, which offered a free service. In August 2018, Amazon merged CreateSpace with its eBook business unit, Kindle Direct Publishing (KDP), which today is widely regarded as the top provider of free paperback and eBook self publishing services. The second company that I decided to use for paperback self publishing was NOOK Press, a unit of Barnes & Noble (B&N). Today, the group is called Barnes & Noble Press. Next, I engaged Ingram Content Group, or Ingram, who offers a self publishing service through its IngramSpark business unit for a one-time fee of, currently, $49 for a paperback and eBook. Back in 2017, I also learned Ingram was the leading provider of books to Libraries, a presence that would bode well for me later. I chose the above three, initially, because of their brand recognition in the self publishing industry and market strength in areas I planned to try to sell my book. Each possessed access to potentially millions of online customers and or thousands of retailers, Libraries, and bookstores. In 2019, Blurb became the fourth company that I use for paperback sales and distribution. Like the other three companies, they too offer eBook services, but I am not using the service at this juncture.

When I was ready to roll out my first eBook, in 2017, I used KDP and enrolled in its KDP Select program, which I will explain in the following eBook Service Provider section. When 2018 rolled around, I noticed more and more successful self publishers and self publishing publications were touting the benefits of an author "going wide" with their service provider approach. I followed suit and began adding additional providers. My decision to "go wide" turned out to be a good one. Not only have my book sales increased, but I've also seen them become more stable than when I was only dealing with two or three providers. Today, as mentioned previously, I am distributing my written works through ten (10) companies. Of the paperback providers, both Amazon and B&N Press offer paperback and eBook services for free. As shared, Ingram offers its paperback service for a fee. If you don't upload your digital book at the same time as your paperback, Ingram's eBook charge is twenty-five ($25) dollars. Blurb requires you to order a proof of your paperback book before they distribute it, which I view as a fee. As of this writing, I have not used Blurb's eBook service, so I don't know if there is a charge involved or not. All of the other service providers that I'm using offer free eBook service. If you don't recognize the names of some of them, neither did I a few years ago. Most are well known in the self publishing arena, however. Next, I'll discuss a few of them.

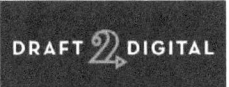  

eBook Service Providers

Smashwords has been in the industry since 2008. On its website, the company states it is "the world's largest distributor of Indie eBooks" and that over 135,000 authors, small independent publishers, and literary agents publish and distribute through them. The company distributes to major online eBook retailers such as Barnes & Noble, Apple Books, Kobo, Tolino, and Libraries via relationships with OverDrive who distributes to over 40,000 Libraries, Baker & Taylor via its Axis 360 platform, Bibliotheca CloudLibrary, Odilo, and Gardners.

Draft2Digital (D2D) distributes to many of the same digital bookstores (i.e., Apple, Kobo, Barnes & Noble, etc.) that

Smashwords does. In an August 2017 Good e-Reader article entitled, "Draft2Digital is the Best Ebook Distribution Platform for Indie Authors," Michael Kozlowski describes D2D as one of the rising superstars Indie Authors should get to know. Also, Dave Chesson of Kindlepreneur in, "SMASHWORDS VS DRAFT2DIGITAL VS PUBLISHDRIVE REVIEW," rates D2D higher than Smashwords and PublishDrive. I agree with Chesson's assessment. I find D2D's website to be much easier to use and navigate than Smashwords, and D2D's process for converting a book into an eBook is far superior. D2D's conversion tool does all of the work for you, whereas, with Smashwords, you have to follow their one hundred seventeen (117) page formatting instructions nearly to the letter for your book to be converted by them into an eBook.

Per PublishDrive's website, publishers and authors have published over 100,000 eBooks with the company, and they offer access to over four hundred (400) online stores and two hundred forty thousand (240,000) Libraries in five continents. I've incorporated PublishDrive as a part of my strategy to expand my books internationally.

Review Your Provider Agreements

When you are deciding on a provider, do take the time to read through their agreements. You may find there's a "catch," if you will, that may prohibit or limit your book sales in some way.

Exclusivity Arrangements

Some of the service provider agreements you will come across might contain exclusivity clauses. Amazon's KDP Select program, for example, is an exclusive offering that opens up your eBook to the Kindle world and provides royalties of up to 70%. Per KDP Select's current Terms and Conditions, "When you include a Digital Book in KDP Select, you give us the exclusive right to sell and distribute your Digital Book in digital format while your book is in KDP Select. During this period of exclusivity, you cannot sell or distribute, or give anyone else the right to sell or distribute, your Digital Book (or a book that is substantially similar), in digital format in any territory where you have rights." Ouch! What this means is, if you want to sell your eBook through Smashwords, D2D, or anyone else for that matter, you can't while you are in the KDP Select program. Currently, the terms of KDP Select require you to stay enrolled in the program for three (3) months at a time.

Afterward, you can opt-out or continue to remain in the program for 3-month intervals. For my first book, I stayed in the program for six (6) months. One of the reasons why it took me so long to begin selling my eBook through other companies was, KDP Select's exclusivity clause had me bound. The other was I didn't realize the benefits of "going wide."

If I had to do it all over again, I would have enrolled in KDP Select for no longer than three months, if at all, for my first book. The reason being, because of non-Amazon providers' market share. In June 2020, eBook.com wrote about Amazon's eBook share of the market. To paraphrase, "The figure varies from 83 percent to considerably less. Our polling of publishers suggests that leaving aside Amazon's publishing efforts and their self-publishing platform, their share of the eBook market sits at 67 percent." So, by being "stuck," if you will, in KDP Select's exclusivity clause, I was not engaging companies that had anywhere from 17-33% eBook market share!

When I learned Ingram distributed to the Apple Books market, I jumped at the opportunity to "sign up." Upon reviewing their eBook agreement, however, I came across an exclusivity "clause," which prohibited selling an eBook through other channels such as Amazon. The clause was Ingram's version of KDP Select, in my view. These types of "catch 22" scenarios, as I call them, are reasons why you should read providers' Terms and Conditions carefully so that you can make a decision that fits your marketing strategy best.

Beware the Sharks

The self publishing industry has become a big business, and where money and growth reside, there are bound to be sharks! Like great whites feasting on unsuspecting prey, there are companies out there who will try to take advantage of new self publishers, particularly during the timeframe when they are building and "packaging" their first books.

In WrittenWordMedia.com's article, "The Top Ten Publishing Industry Trends Every Author Needs to Know in 2020" by Clayton Noblit, the number seven trend was, "Scam services will continue to pop up." Noblit goes on to write, "Unfortunately, this trend will continue in 2020. With self-publishing continuing to grow, more shady characters will be attracted to the money in the market."

So do use resources such as Alli's best and worst list before you dive into an offer that seems too good to be true.

C – Channelize and Market Your Book

Channelize - send from one person or place to another

Preparing Your Book for Service Providers

Now that you've gotten your book written and edited, received your front and back covers from your cover designer, and identified your service providers, you will need to prepare your title for submission to them.

Pricing Your Book

Trying to come up with a price for your book can leave your head spinning if you allow. You might find yourself wondering, "If the price is high, will people buy my book? If it is low, will I be missing out on additional royalty revenue?" There's no need to worry yourself silly about the price of your book because service providers will allow you to change what you are charging at just about any time. Typically, once you make a price change, the update occurs within 24 to 72 hours. With Ingram, price changes become active, the week following your update.

There is a way to come up with the initial price for your book that's relatively easy, I feel. An article I read recommended going onto Amazon.com and reviewing the costs of books in your genre and then set your price similarly. I take it a step further, however. I hone in on the pricing associated with five to ten books in my genre that have a lot of reviews and ratings of 4 or more stars. Next, I scroll down to the bottom of the landing page of each book, looking for the ones that have roughly the same number of pages as my book so that I can make an "apples to apples" price comparison. Lastly, I take the average price of the books that had a similar number of pages, as my book, to come up with my initial selling price. In the following example, I'm taking the average of the sales price of Books 1 and 2.

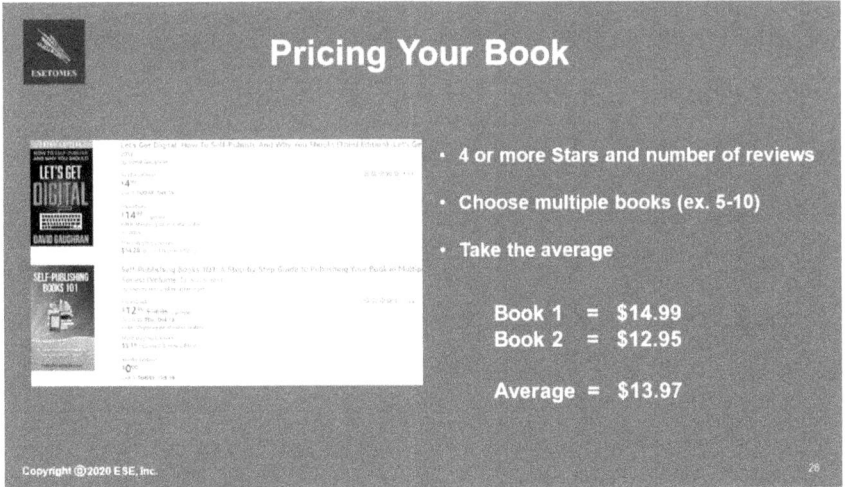

Should you find your sales aren't where you would like for them to be, try changing your price. You can update your pricing with one provider, several, or all of them. I typically change my prices when sales slow down, or for Ad campaigns associated with things like spring break or holidays, for example. Generally, when I make a price change, I submit my update to all of my service providers so that the price for my books is consistent in the marketplace.

Shipping and Handling

One of the things to take into account when you come up with a price for your book is the providers' shipping and handling charges. Let's say it costs $3 for shipping and handling for your $12.79 paperback. The total cost your customer will pay will be $15.79! Initially, when I realized this, it gave me heartburn. Then, I remembered my competitors face the same charges. Strategically, you might decide to lower your price a bit so that it might cost less than your competitors when shipping and handling are added in, or you might choose not to worry about it and just leave your price alone. Either way, just remember shipping and handling costs are out there.

Metadata

Before uploading your book to a self publishing service provider, I highly recommend having your metadata and search words (i.e., keywords) ready in advance. By doing so, you will save yourself time when interacting with the provider's conversion tool, or "platform," which is used to convert your document into a paperback, hardcover, or eBook.

Per IngramSpark in "The Basics of Book Metadata and Keywords," your book's metadata will consist of basic things such as your title, author name, author bio, book description, publication date, etc. Your service providers will also request information on your book's BISAC code, which I will discuss below. Keywords are one or more words used to indicate the content of your title and help make it easier to find your book.

For your bio and book description, I suggest reviewing the biographies and book descriptions of some successful authors to get a feel for the type of information they are presenting to their audience. For the publication date, I typically use the day and year of my final submission to the first service provider that I send my book to for distribution.

BISAC Codes

BISAC subject codes are genre codes, per IngramSpark, and they signal to potential buyers, retailers, distributors, and search engines information on what your book is about, such as the primary genre, topic, or theme. Usually, services providers' platforms allow you to enter up to three BISAC codes. Two of the BISAC codes that I'm using for this book are:

- LAN027000 **LANGUAGE ARTS & DISCIPLINES** / Publishers & Publishing Industry

- LAN025060 / **LANGUAGE ARTS & DISCIPLINES** / Library & Information Science / Digital & Online Resources

I chose codes LAN027000 and LAN025060 because this book deals with both Publishing and Libraries. A website resource that you can use to identify the BISAC code(s) you feel best describes your book, and its content is the Book Industry Study Group's (BISG) page entitled, "Complete BISAC Subject Headings List." The list allows you to drill down on the information so that you can see the various subcategories that might better describe your book.

Keywords

The importance of keywords cannot be overstated because they are the words that will help prospective customers find your book. When thinking about keywords, try to put yourself in your potential buyer's shoes. What search words are they likely to use to find a book such as yours? The search words you come up with should be close to what you think the potential buyer of your title would use.

Some Independent Authors use Amazon.com to develop their keywords. They enter a keyword into Amazon's search bar and use the most popular terms that appear. In contrast, others may use tools like Publisher Rocket, a fee-based tool, in which Nicholas Rossis described as "worth the money" in an October 2019 article for SelfPublishing.com. I recently started using Publisher Rocket for my Amazon Ad campaigns and have found the tool to be helpful, particularly as relates to keywords. One of the benefits of self publishing is, if you feel you aren't having success with your keywords, you can go back and change them.

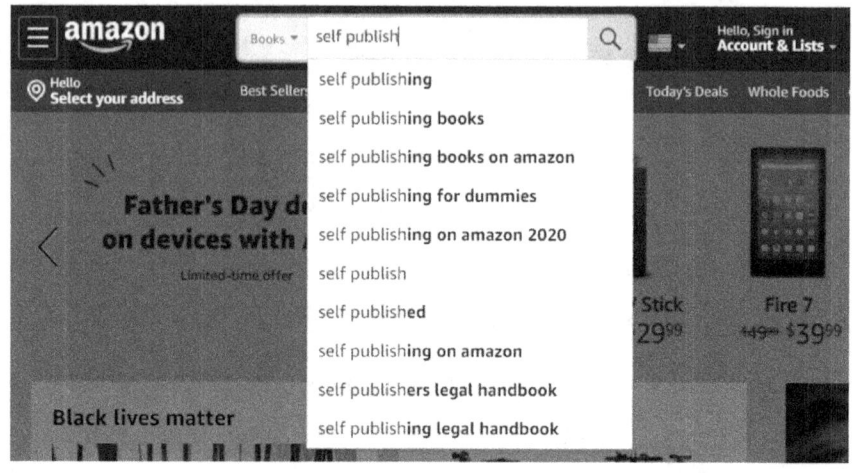

Front, Back, and Spine

Your service providers' "platform" tools will also require you to upload the front, back, and spine (i.e., cover) of your paperback book. I have found using a provider's PDF template to be painstaking when trying to upload the front, back, and spine manually. As a result, I recommend you let your graphic artist or designer know you will need the cover in a format acceptable by KDP for your book's size, such as 6x9 inch, for instance. Once the front, back, and spine make it through KDP's platform, your cover should make it through the other providers' tools as well.

Some of the service providers offer "Cover Creator" tools, which some I've found easy to use and others not so easy. Should you decide to upload your covers manually and utilize a provider's template, make sure it matches your front, back, and spine dimensions.

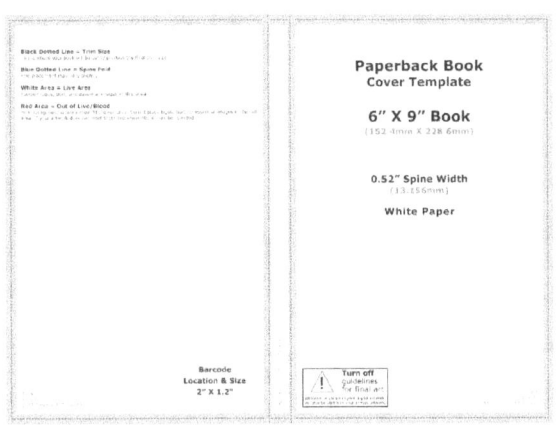

The Submission Process

Although each service provider's platforms are different, the steps in the submission process are similar. They typically involve:

1. **Setup.** In this step, you will upload your book and its cover.
2. **Review.** You will have an opportunity to review the conversion tool's output and make modifications.
3. **Distribute.** Here you will have an opportunity to choose the booksellers and or channels through which you would like your book sold and placed. You'll also provide your book's selling price and metadata.
4. **Convert to eBook.** This step applies more so to providers like Amazon that offer print and eBook services.

Print Book

A few years ago, most self publishing service providers' "platforms" required book submissions to be in PDF format. Today, while many providers still accept PDFs, most will allow you to provide your title to them in Microsoft Word document format. The "setup" usually involves two steps. The first is the uploading of your book's front, spine, and back covers. The second is the uploading of your book, which you might also be able to "drag and drop" into the provider's "platform." If a problem occurs during either step, you will receive an error message. You'll have to correct any errors for your book to be successfully submitted. Once the submission process has been completed, you will be provided a draft, usually in the form of a PDF document, for review. When you're satisfied with the output, you will authorize your provider to begin printing and distributing your book!

eBook – MOBI and ePub Formats

There are various types of eBook formats. Some of the most popular ones are ePub, MOBI, AZW, and PDF. I'll address the two you'll probably run across the most with your providers. They are MOBI and ePub. I view these two formats as analogous to the operating systems used in cellphones MOBI is like Apple's iOS, a proprietary, or "closed" architecture in computer vernacular. In contrast, ePub is like Android, an "open" architecture. MOBI is the eBook format used by Amazon for its Kindle devices, and ePub, which is regarded by some experts as the most popular of the two, is used by Apple, KOBO, Barnes & Noble, and other non-Kindle devices.

You will discover, there is a significant difference between the format of a printed book and an eBook. In "Similarities and Differences Between Print Books and Ebooks," ebooklaunch.com, to paraphrase, states, "The single most important difference is that print books have static layouts that once printed do not change, whereas eBooks have dynamic layouts and are formatted with re-flowable text. Re-flowable text is the ability to automatically wrap words in a document to the next line as the user changes the window size and thereby relocates the right margin of the page."

KDP's platform takes care of converting your print book to the MOBI format for you. To get your book into the ePub format for other providers' platforms, you will have to either use their tool, which is usually pretty straight forward or in Smashwords' current case, manually format your title to their specifications. As shared earlier, Smashwords' instructions for converting your book to ePub format on their platform, is a one hundred (100) page plus document. In its most simplistic form, three key things need to be done to get your book into an acceptable ePub format for Smashwords, I feel. The first is the setting of the first-line indent, for new paragraphs, at about 0.25 inches. Second, if you're using Microsoft Word, is you will need to "bookmark" the sections of your book that you would like to appear in the Table of Contents. And third, in the Table of Contents, you will need to link the related chapter or section to its bookmark. Beyond that, the instructions deal with formatting, which I suggest you keep "vanilla." Admittedly, I've found once a book is formatted to Smashword's eBook specifications, it will pass through other providers' platforms with flying colors.

In my view, Draft2Digital's ePub conversion tool is the easiest to use, and its output is the "best looking" to me, format-wise, of all the providers that I'm using. On one occasion, the PDF review document I received from D2D did not have the company's free ISBN embedded. I was able to use Microsoft Word's ability to convert the PDF to a Word document. Afterward, I had an "ISBN free" or "clean" manuscript generated by a platform tool that I could upload to other platforms. The reason I share this with you is that most of the conversion tools do an excellent job of cleaning up formatting issues you may have missed. Consequently, these tools' output is usually better than your submission. So, if you get lucky and receive a "clean" PDF document to review, once you convert it to Word, it should pass most platforms' conversion process.

On the Internet, you will be able to find free ePub conversion tools, which I would caution you about using. I tried using one from a supposedly legitimate company, and shortly after converting one of my books, I discovered it had been pirated and was being sold on the World Wide Web without my permission. I ended up engaging Google to get the matter resolved. Should something similar happen to you, I've provided the link to Google's Copyright Infringement page in this book's "Reference" section.

Google

Copyright Removal

Report alleged copyright infringement: Web Search

It is our policy to respond to notices of alleged infringement that comply with the Digital Millennium Copyright Act applicable intellectual property laws. Our response may include removing or disabling access to material claimed response to such a notice, we may notify the owner or administrator of the affected site or content so that he or s which we act, including by sending a copy of the notice to one or more third parties or making it available to the p

Infringement Notification

To file a notice of infringement with us, you may use the form provided below.

IMPORTANT: Misrepresentations made in your notice regarding whether material or activity is infringing may exp consider copyright defenses, limitations or exceptions before sending a notice. In one case involving online conte the U.S. fair use doctrine. Accordingly, if you are not sure whether material available online infringes your copyrig

Required field

Contact Information

First name: *

Last name: *

Company Name

You will also be able to find free ePub conversion software available online. Of the companies I've investigated, Calibre is typically the most touted. The product can convert a Word document to ePub, MOBI, and other formats. I have used Calibre for ePub conversion, and the only problem I've run into, on a few occasions, has been having an image or two get turned sideways. Once I found the software feature, which wasn't in a logical place to me, to correct the problem, I was able to resolve my issue.

You'll discover there are numerous tools available to help you convert your book to ePub format. As they continue to evolve, they are becoming more user friendly. Should you find yourself having difficulty with an ePub conversion, there are companies listed on the Internet that offer assistance for a fee. I do think a free downloadable converter, like Calibre, can help you avoid the expense, however.

After service providers have prepared your paperback and eBook for distribution to booksellers, book stores, Libraries, etc., their timeframes vary as to when your book will be available for sale. Some of the providers with online stores, such as Amazon and Barnes & Noble, state it will take 24 to 72 hours before your book will be available for sale. ePubs tend to process rather quickly, but I've seen it take as long as a week for my eBooks to reach all of the end sellers in a provider's channel.

Chapter 2
Marketing Your Book

Now that your service providers have submitted your book to retailers, bookstores, Libraries, and other booksellers that they work with, what comes next? It is up to you to put a plan in place, if you haven't done so already, to begin marketing and promoting your book. So, where do you start?

Determine Your Target Markets

Envision the sales opportunity for your book as if it were an iceberg. The visible part would represent 10% of your possibilities, and the area beneath the surface would be 90%! Using this analogy, family and friends make up the tip of your sales opportunity. While they are the most readily available purchasers after your title has been released, they represent just a small fraction of your overall sales potential. Your "hidden" opportunity lies in those areas "beneath" the surface, and this is where you should "target" your book, and spend the bulk of your time. The following image shows some of the "target" markets and a demographic I chose for my first book.

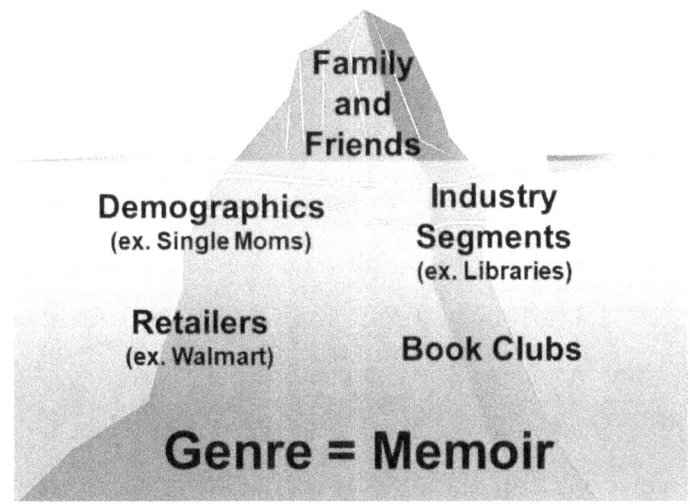

Creating Awareness

Now that you've determined who your "target audience" will be, you will need to come up with a plan as to how you will make them aware of your book. I recommend, at a minimum, you have a website plus a Facebook and Twitter business page for your book to help you create awareness and discoverability.

Website

There are many ways for you to get an Author's website built to promote your book. You can hire someone to set up your site, like me, a Certified Webmaster, or if you're comfortable with technology, you can use a website development platform from companies such as Wix or WordPress. When budgeting for a site, be sure to look at your overall cost. Your site will need to be "hosted" and maintained by someone, if not yourself. Also, there might be charges involved from your website provider for adding news articles and blog information that you might want to have on your site. I suggest you visit various Authors' websites to get an idea about the type of content they have on their sites so that you can begin to formulate thoughts for your site. Feel free to take a look at my site's content at www.eseinc1.com/esetomes-books.

Engaging Your Target Markets

Before engaging your target markets, think about who, what, when, where, why, and how. I'll use a few of the lessons I've learned from engaging Libraries, one of my target markets, to illustrate. At the onset, I didn't know **Who** Libraries purchased their books from and **How** they made their buying decisions. Upon doing some research, I came across an American Library Association page entitled "Frequently Asked Questions from Authors and Publishers." It mentioned, "Libraries purchase books through such companies as Baker & Taylor, Ingram Library Services, Emery-Pratt Company, and other book suppliers and wholesalers." These companies were the **Who** I was looking for regarding the sources from which Libraries purchase their books. This information also helped me to decide on using Ingram as one of my service providers. Later, I learned **Who** makes the purchasing decisions at a Library. Depending upon the size of a facility, it could be the Head Librarian or the Collections/Acquisition Manager. Once I began engaging Librarians, some would refer me to their "Collection Development Policy," which is the guideline as to **How** a Library makes its purchasing decisions. My research also provided me with information as to **When** Libraries procure. Although many buy throughout the year, I have found contacting Librarians several months before their Fiscal Year End and Fiscal Year Begin, which for many is in the June/July timeframe, is a good time to get a book in front of them.

Using the example above, try to learn as much as you can about your target audience. The knowledge that you acquire will help you in developing effective marketing strategies for them.

Advertising

To stir up interest before I release a book, I try to put out an advertising "teaser" on Facebook, Twitter, and my website, at least one week in advance of the book becoming widely available. The "teaser" might include the front cover of the book with a caption overhead that reads, "Coming Soon!" Shortly afterward, I will begin running, on all three sites, a forty-five (45) second, or so, "Infomercial," that I have created. I use a product called Wondershare Filmora9, a video editing software package that can be downloaded for free, to create my social media and website "Infomercial." Back in 2017, I purchased a "lifetime" license of the software for $59.99 because I would also be using it for my website business and didn't want the Filmora watermark appearing on my videos, which is not the case, I believe, with the free version. Designed for beginners and casual users, Filmora9 gives me the capability to take a PowerPoint presentation that I've created, announcing my book, and turn it into a video. In addition to my website and social media business pages, I also put the "Infomercial" on YouTube.

Should you choose, you could also run pre and post book release Ad campaigns, that you provide, on Amazon, Facebook, Twitter, and Instagram for a fee. Where available, I tend to run "pay per click" type Ads in which you only get charged when someone clicks on your Ad. My recommendation is that you establish a low budget and try running ads on the above sites to see what impact they have on your sales, before spending a significant dollar amount on online advertising. I primarily use Amazon now for my Ads because their "real-time" reporting shows sales that have been generated by an Ad campaign, which in turn helps in assessing an Ad's effectiveness. With social media advertising, there isn't a way that I know of, to determine whether or not an Ad is contributing to sales because these sites aren't directly tied to online book retailers' purchasing systems, as Amazon Advertising is to Amazon.com. The upside to social media advertising, however, is the large number of people to which your book can be exposed.

    You can also pay for Ads through some of your service providers, or through other sources, you feel will help you get the word out about your book. Ultimately, you should strive to get to a point where the revenue from your book's sales can be used to pay for your future Ads. Because advertising and promotion will probably be your more significant expenses, after your title has been released, you will want to be sure to manage these expenditures in a way that will get you the most bang for your buck.

Chapter 3
Setting up Your Book Business

At some point, preferably before you've finished your book and submitted it to service providers, you will want to consider setting up a business for your book. It doesn't have to be anything elaborate, but you will need some type of "business" structure in place, if for no other reason than for tax purposes. It's important to remember when your book is sold, each sale is reported as revenue to the IRS by the selling party. IRS Publication 525 (2019), Taxable and Nontaxable Income (Rev. February 2020) in the Royalties section states, "Royalties from copyrights on literary, musical, or artistic works, and similar property, or from patents on inventions, are amounts paid to you for the right to use your work over a specified period of time. Royalties are generally based on the number of units sold, such as the number of books, tickets to a performance, or machines sold." I couldn't find where the IRS states what the number of units sold is bookwise that becomes taxable, but KDP's website says Amazon global royalties over $10 are subject to taxes. So, the takeaway is, if you've met the "threshold," you should receive a 1099-MISC, according to KDP. I exceeded the threshold on each of my books in 2019 and didn't receive a 1099-MISC from any provider, however. This lack of receipt leads me to believe the criteria revolves around units sold. Should you have questions about taxation on your royalties, do contact your service provider.

When you are setting up your account with a service provider, they will request information from you, such as your Taxpayer ID or your social security number, business type, the bank account number that you want your royalties to go to, and the like. From a "type of business" standpoint, I chose to Incorporate to protect my assets. You can set up a Sole Proprietorship, Limited Liability Company (LLC), or some other business type you feel will work best for you. If you need help with your decision, do seek advice from an accountant, or similar, to get an understanding of the advantages and disadvantages of each business type.

For the management of your business' accounting, there is software available such as QuickBooks or free online services such as Wave, which is what I use, which can help you keep track of your revenues, expenses, p&l (i.e., profit and loss), etc. Expense-wise, there is one tax deduction that might get easily overlooked by self publishers, and it is their mileage expense, which can add up quickly, especially when one is traveling to and from events such as book signings. To give you an idea of the impact of the deduction, in 2017, I drove 4,346 business miles for my website and book business. The way the IRS calculated business mileage at the time, my mileage expense deduction for the year turned out to be around $2,000! I used an app called Hurdlr, which cost sixty dollars ($60) at the time, to track my mileage. I certainly felt I got a good return on my investment in the app. There are numerous apps out there to help you with mileage tracking, so do look into one if you anticipate doing a good bit of book-related travel.

Chapter 4
Managing Your Book Business

Ultimately, how you choose to run and manage your book business will depend on your "management" style, time, and other factors. I tend to keep a close eye on my "Book Business." In this chapter, I'll share with you for your consideration, some of the things I'm doing to help me manage and stay on top of my book business.

Book Database

I maintain an Excel spreadsheet, which I refer to as my "Book Database." It is a repository of information in which I keep the following and other data:

- Service provider sales results
- Provider ISBN for each book
- Current pricing for each title
- Advertising, book orders, and other expenses
- Service provider royalties
- Profit/Loss

I have the "Database" set up in such a way that when I record a provider's "number of units sold," my royalties are automatically calculated. I use my sales figures to keep track of how my books are doing revenue-wise and as an "audit tool" to ensure my service providers are correctly disbursing my royalty payments. I'm also able to keep track of my overall profit/loss with my books. At the end of the year, I can then reconcile any differences between my spreadsheet and what's in the Wave accounting system.

The reason why I am so meticulous about my "book business" and its numbers is because I'm chasing profitability, which is something I think might be an afterthought with many self publishers. Many of our peers seem to be focused on tracking volume sales. What good does it do if you sell 10,000 copies of your book, but you lose $5,000 in doing so, I ask? Instead, I seek to make a financial return on the tremendous amount of investment (i.e., blood, sweat, tears, and revenue) I have put into my books. As a result, my goal is to have all of my titles, when combined, be profitable in my third year of selling my written works, which just so happens to be this year (2020). By all accounts, I will meet my profitability objective by the end of the year. I doubt many self publishers can say they were profitable by year three. As a consequence, I strongly recommend you focus on profit early on.

Whether you use your accounting software or build a "Book Database" as a sales and royalty cross-checker, having some type of "system" in place will help you manage your "book business" more efficiently. If you would like more information about my "Book Database," feel free to reach out to me on my website at https://www.eseinc1.com/esetomes-books.

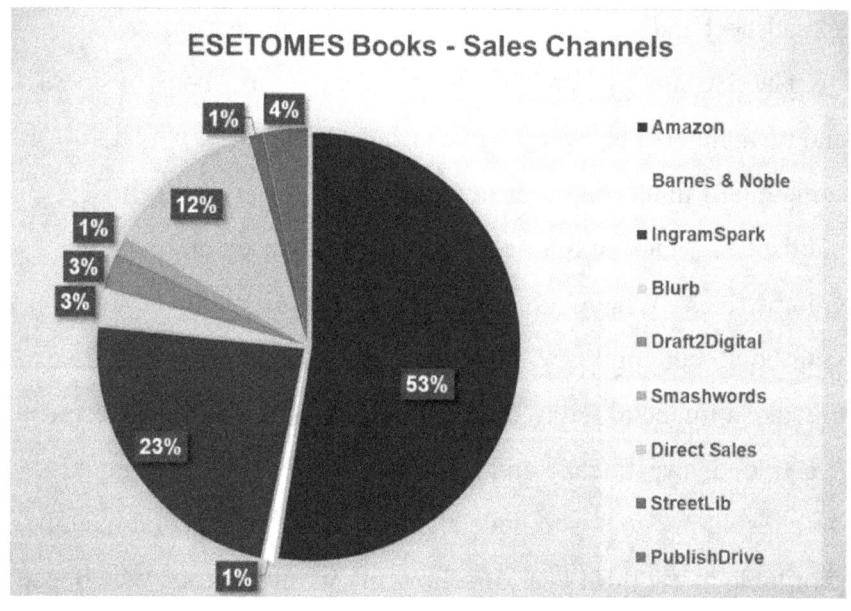

RSS Feed

An RSS feed is an excellent resource to help you manage updates to your social media platforms, almost simultaneously, from one source. RSS stands for Rich Site Summary and is often called Really Simple Syndication. Wikipedia defines RSS feed as a web feed that allows users and applications to access updates to websites in a standardized, computer-readable format.

With an RSS feed, you can write a blog on your Author's website and have it transmitted, via the feed, to a social media automation tool provider, who, in turn, transmits the blog to your Facebook, Twitter, and Instagram business pages. I use a company by the name of dlvr.it for my social media automation. I've found the ability to update my social media business pages using automation, versus doing so manually, to be a tremendous time-saver. Most website providers (Wix, WordPress, etc.) have RSS feed capability. You can visit dlvr.it's website to learn more about the company, or Google, "dlvr.it Alternatives & Competitors," to find out information about other companies that offer social media automation solutions.

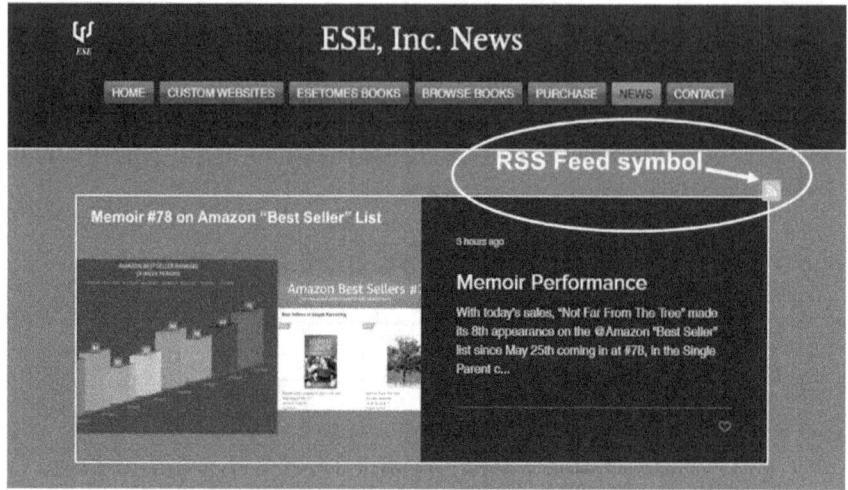

Browser Bookmarks

For sites that you will frequently be visiting, such as ones containing your providers' sales reports, bookmark those pages so that they will be readily accessible to you.

Now that you have your book out in the marketplace, you will need to begin implementing your "awareness" strategy for the "target" market(s) you've decided to pursue so that you can start familiarizing its audience(s) with your title. Convinced Libraries are a viable "target" market for you to go after right away, in the following sections, I'll share with you the methodology I've developed to get my self published books into ninety-eight (98) Libraries, as of this writing, around the world in just over two years.

I'll make mention of one or more of my titles from time to time to illustrate how I have marketed that particular book(s) to Libraries.

Chapter 5
Marketing Your Book to Libraries

Why Libraries?

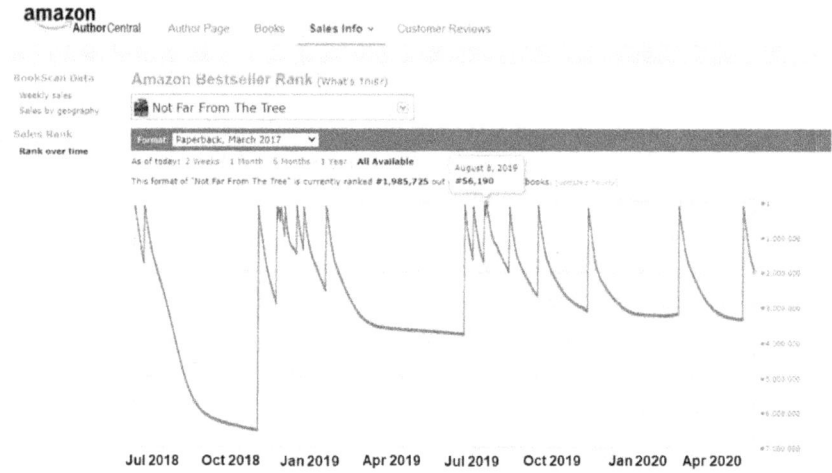

ESETOMES Retail and Library Sales Mirroring One Another

Whenever I would observe my Amazon sales of *Not Far From The Tree* during its first nine (9) months in the marketplace, one thing was painfully clear. It was, my sales were like a rollercoaster. After deciding in December 2017 that I would begin focusing on Libraries as a "target" market, the following January, I initiated my first Library email campaign. As my marketing efforts increased, I began to receive orders for my book from Academic Libraries, the segment of the market I had decided to focus on first. Around July 2019 and following, several exciting things began to happen. One was, and as the previous image shows, the considerable "gaps" in which I had little to no sales, began to narrow once my Library marketing efforts started to kick in. Another was my Amazon retail sales started mirroring my Library sales! Now, whenever my Library sales go up, the same tends to happen with my Amazon consumer transactions. Also, the states in which I've had Library sales mirror those in which I've had Amazon retail sales. The exception being, consumers have made purchases in four (4) additional states. I've yet to figure out the correlation between my Library and consumer sales. My guess is people who have borrowed my books from Libraries are buying them afterward, which would validate a study that revealed forty percent (40%) of people who checked out a book from a Library ended up purchasing the book.

July was also the time frame in which my Library sales began to pick up dramatically. Seventy-two percent (72%) of Libraries' purchases of my books have occurred since. I attribute purchases by two award-winning Libraries for helping jump-start more frequent acquisitions of my books, and particularly my Memoir, by other Libraries. Howard County Library System (HCLS), Library

Journal's **2013 Library of The Year**, ordered three (3) copies of my Memoir during the month, and Stark County District Library, a Journal 2018 "**Star Library**," ordered two copies.

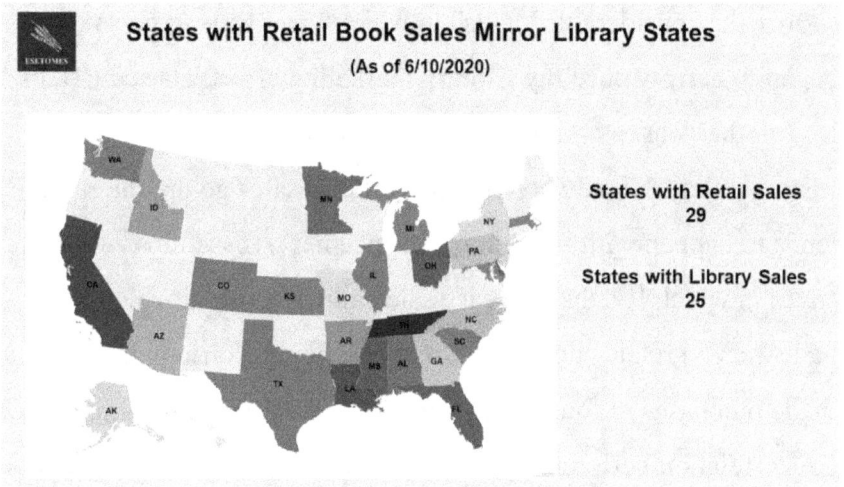

Why I Chose the Library Segment

Long before I had finished self publishing my first book, I knew I wanted to establish near irrefutable credibility around the title with potential purchasers. My decision to go after Libraries as a "target market" was due in large part to the trustworthiness people tend to associate with these facilities, and because they have what's called a "Collection Development Policy." Per its website, the New Orleans Public Library, one of my customers, states, "The Collection

Development Policy is designed to support the Library's Mission statement and serves as a guide for the selection, acquisition, maintenance, and retention of materials."

Having a book in a library, I feel, can help establish an Author's credibility with prospective readers because the book has been vetted by and passed a "litmus" test, so to speak, with Librarians for the work to be considered for purchase and placement within their facility. Also, Libraries are highly "referenceable" customers for an Author, especially with other Libraries. It has been my experience when you get your book into one Library; the odds go up dramatically that others are likely to follow. I call this the "Domino Effect," and I believe it's occurring with my customers. To illustrate, after initiating a "Library Campaign" in January 2018, Washington University in St. Louis became the first Library to purchase my Memoir. With this "highly referenceable" account, I have been able to get twenty-two other Academic Libraries to place orders for the book as well. When I began focusing on Public Libraries, the Detroit Public Library, the 12th largest in the Nation, became my first customer in the segment. They ordered two copies of my Memoir for two Branches. Fast forward to today, and seventy-one (71) additional Public Libraries, and three (3) Library Services Companies have ordered my three previous books.

Each time a Library purchases one of my titles, I add them to my "Reference List" (https://www.esetomes.com/library-customers), and I share the list with prospective Libraries in my introductory letters and marketing campaigns. When I was "fine-tuning" my correspondence to Librarians, I ran several campaigns in which I provided the link to my "Reference List." Later, my Google Analytics data showed just a few Librarians were clicking on the URL, so I went back to inserting the "List" in my emails.

One clear benefit I have seen from providing Library references is a shorter time to sales closure, particularly with Public Libraries, which, in my case, is now down from a six-month purchase cycle to three months, on average. I've also had twenty (20) Libraries to date that have purchased after one email contact!

The Library Market

Before its discontinuance, a prototype developed by the Online Computer Library Center (OCLC) revealed, there were 1.4 million Libraries worldwide, and of these 336,841 were Academic and Public (45,028 and 291,813 respectively) facilities. In the U.S., the data showed 3,094 Academic and 9,057 Public libraries, which closely mirrors the American Library Association's (ALA) numbers. I view the Public Library "Market Opportunity" in the

U.S. as 16,568, however, which is the total number of buildings per ALA. In June 2020, the International Federation of Library Associations and Institution's (IFLA) "Library Map of The World" showed the number of Libraries worldwide had grown to 2.6 million. Of these, there were 94,677 Academic and 405,791 Public Libraries around the globe (500,468 total). If your focus is going to be on School Libraries (Public, Private, and Bureau of Indian Affairs), the Map showed there were 2.1 million such Libraries around the world. In the U.S., ALA's figures showed there were 98,460 School Libraries, which is eight (8) times the number of Public and Academic Libraries in the country combined! As you can see, the Library market is enormous!

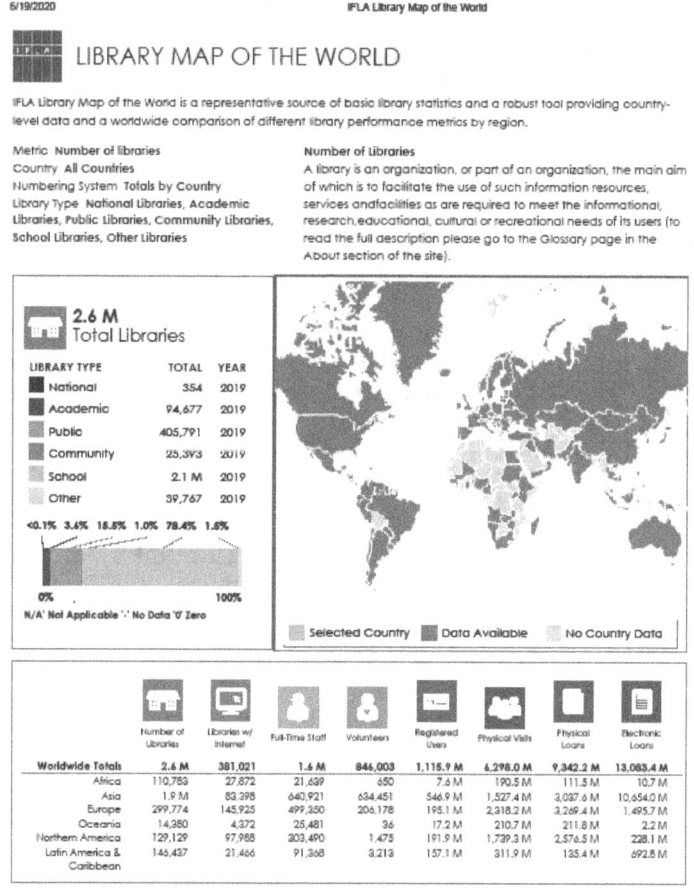

(*Downloadable image courtesy of IFLA*)

If you are targeting millennials for your book, they are more likely than older generations to say Libraries help them find trustworthy information, learn new things, and make informed decisions, per a 2016 Pew Research Center survey.

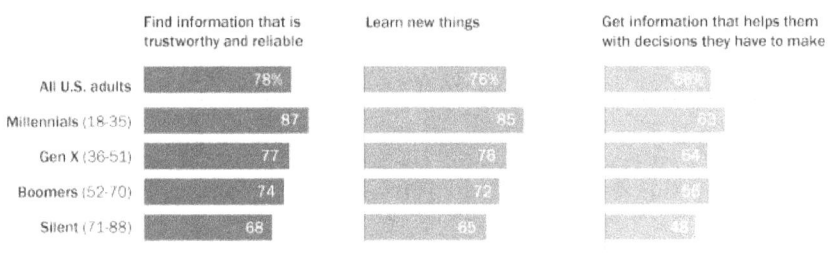

(*Downloadable image courtesy of Pew Research Center*)

On February 22, 2017, Reedsy published an article, "5 Reasons Why Selling to Libraries Needs to be a Top Priority," which stated, " ... 92% of librarians surveyed between May 2016 – July 2016 by New Shelves noted that they regularly buy books from self published authors and small presses. The article goes on to say, "Once one library has your book and the check-out rates start showing up on reports, other librarians will start ordering your book. The growth and spread of your book's sales and popularity will start happening while you are not even looking!"

The Challenge

While reviews aren't necessarily a requirement to get your self published book into many Libraries, you will find some Librarians still rely heavily on book reviews. One sent me the following email. "New library materials are considered for purchase using a variety of selection criteria including favorable reviews in standard library review media (Library Journal, Kirkus, Booklist), anticipated demand for the material, local interest, and space and budgetary considerations."

Admittedly, I struggle mightily with book reviews. Here's why. Per Kirkus' website, and as of this writing, the charge for a "Traditional Review" is $425 U.S., and you can expect a 250-300 word review back in 7-9 weeks. If you want your review expedited, the cost is $575. A second option is an "Expanded Review" that can be received in 7-9 weeks for $575, and for an expedited review, the cost is $725. At a royalty rate of let's say, $3.00 U.S. for a paperback book, one would have to sell roughly one hundred forty-two (142) books to break even on the "Traditional Review." That's like giving 142 Libraries a book for free! At this juncture, I prefer not to "pay to play," if you will, to get my works into Libraries because the fees are more than I'm currently willing to pay. Thanks, but no thanks!! I do realize, however, my stubbornness could be costing me revenue. Let's assume a Kirkus "Traditional Review" yielded me, 1,000 new Library customers. Using the previous $3.00 royalty rate, I might be missing out on a net revenue gain of $2,575 ($3,000-$425).

In my article, "How To Get Your Book Into Libraries," for the CreativePenn.com, I mentioned I was staying pat on paying for a book review. My position was based on Kirkus' cost and my "marketing" budget at the time. About six months after the article had been posted, Publishers Weekly (PW) announced a Fiction and Nonfiction Contest called The BookLife Prize that had a grand prize of $5,000, and the entry fee was $99. BookLife is a Publishers Weekly site dedicated to Indie Authors. On the website, Authors can submit their self published books to PW for review consideration, or they can purchase a BookLife Review for $399. Booklife's review is advertised as being a complete review written by an expert Publishers Weekly reviewer, that will be returned in roughly six weeks. For the contest, however, the entrants were to receive a brief critical assessment of their manuscript written by a Publishers Weekly reviewer. Because of the low entry fee, I decided to enter *Not Far From The Tree* into the contest. Nine weeks, and not six, later, I received my book's assessment. While there were comments that I appreciated and constructive criticism that I did not object to, the review document looked canned. Furthermore, it was pretty apparent to me; the reviewer had only read a few sections of the book. Perhaps I was expecting too much for my $99, but a review that came three weeks later than stated and one in which it seemed my book was not read in its entirety, left me feeling as though I had wasted my money.

Book Review Resources

Should you opt for a book review, before you start engaging Libraries, the following list of resources provided by IngramSpark, should help. Keep in mind many of these publications require submission before a book's publication.

- Booklist: Adult and Youth | Circulation: 80,000 print; 160,000 online
- Library Journal: Adult | Circulation: 100,000
- Library Journal Self-e program: Adult and Youth self-published eBooks
- Publishers Weekly and PW Children's: Adult and Youth | Circulation: 25,000
- School Library Journal: Youth titles | Circulation: 33,000 print; 44,000 online

- Voice of Youth Advocates (VOYA): Young Adult | Circulation: 7,000
- Choice Magazine: Academic | Circulation: 22,000 librarians and faculty
- The Bulletin of the Center for Children's Books: Youth | Circulation: 2,000
- Horn Book: Youth | Circulation: 13,000
- Kirkus Reviews: Adult and Youth | Circulation: 3,000 print

I would also suggest you keep an eye out for "review" discounts from one of the above entities.

Chapter 6
Getting Started Marketing to Libraries

The pursuit of getting your book into Libraries will require some strategy development on your part. Before getting started, you'll need to know at least two things. 1). Who the primary decision-makers are in the Libraries that you'll be contacting, and 2). Where these Libraries tend to go to purchase their books.

Key Decision-Makers in a Library

Depending on the size of a Library, the key decision-makers will have titles such as Head Librarian, Director, Branch Manager, or in the case of Academic Libraries, perhaps Dean. Other vital titles are Collection Development Librarian or Acquisitions Librarian. If it's a sizeable Library, don't be surprised if the Collection Development Librarian has the latitude to make the final decision on a book purchase. This individual carries a lot of weight, and quite often, the Head Librarian will refer you to the Collections Development Librarian. You should also look for potential "influencers" in a Library. If a Librarian has responsibility for children's books, and you've written one, that person needs to be on your contact list.

Also, look for Librarians' genre responsibility such as Adult Books, as well. When marketing to Libraries, I've found the best approach to be "**top-down**" and "**bottom-up**" selling. In other words, sell to the top decision-maker in the Library and those lower down in the decision-making chain, such as a Branch Manager who might be an influential recommender. Approaching your selling efforts in this fashion allows you to "cover more bases." Let's say you send a Head Librarian information about your book, and they don't make the purchasing decision. More than likely, they'll pass it on to the person that does. If so, the Head Librarian might simply ask the purchasing decision-maker to take a look at your book, or they might say your title is worth adding to the Library's Collection, which in this case would be an order request to the purchasing decision-maker. When you send information about your manuscript to a Library's Branch Manager, they might inform you the Library System's purchasing is centralized. If the Branch Manager feels your book would be a good fit for their location, however, they might put in a purchasing request to their central location. Taking this example a step further, if multiple Branch Managers request your book, the System's Purchasing Department might end up placing an order for multiple copies, which has happened to me at least nine (9) times!

For large Libraries, try to have at least two or more contacts. Also, if you find information in a non-decision-making Librarian's bio that makes you think they might purchase your book for their leisurely reading, do contact them as well. In reviewing a University's Library contacts once, I noticed a Professor, who assisted the Library, had mentioned she enjoyed reading memoirs. I sent her information about my book. Later, not only did the University end up ordering a copy of my title, the Professor purchased a copy for herself as well!

How Do Libraries Select Books?

While Libraries' Collection Development Policies may differ, based on a variety of factors such as Patron demographics, etc., the American Library Association (ALA) has "suggested guidelines" if you will, for Public, School, and Academic Libraries in a document entitled, "Selection Criteria" (http://www.ala.org/tools/challengesupport/selectionpolicytoolkit/criteria). While not all-inclusive, I've listed some of ALA's criteria that stand out to me as a self publisher.

General Criteria

- Suitability of subject and style for the intended audience
- Exhibit a high degree of potential user appeal and interest
- Scope and content
- Meet high standards in literary, artistic, and aesthetic quality; technical aspects; and physical format

Content Criteria

- Skill, competence, and purpose of the author
- Vitality and originality
- Clarity
- Sustained interest

I believe if an Author understands where their book fits within a Library's Collection Development Policy, they can use that knowledge to show Librarians how their title aligns with the Policy. To illustrate, I reside in Metro Atlanta, and I wanted to get my Memoir into every Library in the Fulton County Library System, which has thirty-four Branches. Cognizant Atlanta proper has a sizeable minority population; I sought to educate myself on the System's Collection Development Policy as relates to diversity. Upon reading the material, one section stated, "The library will, therefore, seek to acquire, organize, disseminate, and preserve information resources that are both relevant to the advancement of human knowledge in general and specific to the particular needs of our diverse, metropolitan community." Following, I did some demographic research to build a case showing why my Memoir would be a good fit for the System's "diverse" community. As a part of my "value proposition," I created a map (see the following image) of the cities of Public Libraries that had purchased my book and whose demographics were similar to Atlanta's. My subsequent email Subject line read, "Demographics of Libraries Purchasing *Not Far From The Tree* Mirror Atlanta." In my correspondence, I shared my research revealed the purchasing Public Libraries had, on average, a 37% African American Population as compared to Atlanta's 38%."

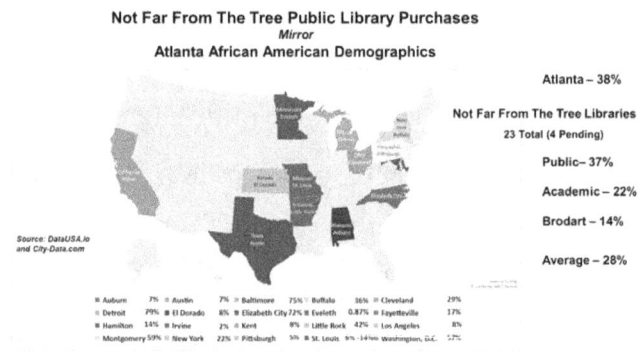

After two years of trying to get my Memoir into Fulton County, the System purchased the eBook version of the title shortly after receipt of my "justification" letter. I'm convinced showing how my manuscript aligned with the System's Collection Development Policy around diversity is what helped closed the deal. Now that I have my "foot in the door," and with the System as a reference, I believe my odds of getting each Branch to buy a paperback copy have gone up dramatically.

Now, I don't go into as much in-depth research for every Library as I did for Fulton County, but if a System has ten or more Branches, I might. So the key take away is, if you can show how your book aligns with a Library's Collection Development Policy, your chances for getting your book into a Library, should increase.

Where Do Libraries Go to Purchase Their Books?

Libraries purchase their books from a variety of sources. Two of the most widely used are Ingram Content Group, or Ingram, and Baker & Taylor (B&T), both of whom I mentioned earlier in the Book Distributors section. Per Wikipedia, Ingram has the industry's most extensive active book inventory with access to 7.5 million titles, and the markets they serve include booksellers, Librarians, educators, and specialty retailers. As also mentioned earlier,

IngramSpark, a division of Ingram, differs from free self publishing platforms in that it has a setup fee of $49 per print book, currently, or $49 for print and eBook when uploaded at the same time, or $25 for an eBook if submitted separately. According to its website, Baker & Taylor is a premier provider of books, digital content, and technology solutions that help Public Libraries improve community outcomes through literacy and learning. Some of the other resources Libraries procure from and that I'm using, include Amazon, via KDP's Expanded Distribution offering, Smashwords, Draft2Digital, and StreetLib. Blurb, who I'm also using, distributes through Ingram, so they should be able to reach Libraries as well.

Currently, sixty percent (60%) of my Library sales come from Ingram, and fifteen percent (15%) come from KDP's Expanded Distribution offering. The remaining twenty-five percent (25%) comes from the other service providers mentioned above. Three years ago, Baker & Taylor seemed to be preferred by many Librarians, but I've not noticed lately, my B&T sales have slowed.

On the eBook side of the equation, you'll find Libraries tend to purchase from digital content providers such as OverDrive, B&T, via its Axis 360 platform, Hoopla, and Bibliotheca, to name a few. After a Library has purchased your eBook, it will be available for their Patrons to download for free.

According to AmericanLibrariesMagazine.org, OverDrive is the largest commercial provider of eBooks and other digital content to Libraries. Serving more than 43,000 Libraries, OverDrive is the market share leader, and more than 95% of Public Libraries in the U.S. and Canada rely on it for digital lending and other services. From a royalties perspective, Libraries lend eBooks like physical books are done, and as a result, you get paid once, by a service provider, for an eBook Library purchase. D2D, however, also offers OverDrive's Cost Per Checkout (CPC) payment option in which you can get compensated every time your eBook is checked out! D2D says about the Cost Per Checkout, "CPC allows Libraries to have access to the same title for more than one user. Instead of a fixed price, Libraries gain access to your books and pay 1/10 of the book's full purchase price, each time it is loaned out." To date, I've only had one CPC transaction, but should Library funding drop significantly after COVID-19, I can see more and more Libraries going to the model.

Chapter 7
Building Your "Library Contacts Database"

To be able to keep track of and manage your activities with Libraries, you'll need some type of tool or resource to help you stay on top of things. Aside from you and your books, this "tool" will be your most valuable asset in helping facilitate your success in marketing to Libraries. To help me engage Libraries, I created a resource that I refer to as my Library Contacts "Database." I view it as "invaluable," and without it, I'm convinced I would not have been able to close as many Library sales as I have.

I used Microsoft Excel to build my "Database." Today, it contains four thousand three hundred seventy-eight (4,378) Libraries (1,288 Academic and 3,090 Public) and has over five thousand (5,000) Library contacts. In the spreadsheet, I keep separate tabs for my Academic and Public Libraries because this makes it easier for me to do "targeted" mass mailings to either sector. The "Database" has the following field headings:

- **Status** (so I can input whether I've checked to see if a Library has purchased one of my books)

- **State**
- **Library Type** (i.e., Public or Academic)
- **Library Link** (i.e., URL)
- **First Name**
- **Last Name**
- **Salutation** (example Mary, or Dr. Smith)
- **Email Address**
- **Date Contacted**
- **Library Name**
- **Notes**

In the Notes field, I put the name of the consortium, if the Library belongs to one so that I can email all of the group's members during a "targeted" marketing campaign. The same applies to Library Systems, with a large number of Branches.

When I decided on Libraries as a "target" segment, my initial goal was to introduce my book to America's biggest Libraries. I started by Googling, "largest libraries in the United States." The top search result was "List of the Largest Libraries in the United States – Wikipedia." When I went to the page, I found several lists that I copied and pasted into a spreadsheet that would later become my Library Contacts "Database." Next, I went onto each Library's website and searched for their decision-makers. This one by one method of finding contact information proved to be a long and arduous process. I knew there had to be a better way. Over time, I discovered some states list their Libraries and Library Directors on the state's government website. These contacts might be available via a downloadable spreadsheet or PDF document. On a few occasions, I found, just sitting out on the Internet, some Excel spreadsheets that were several years old, that had all of the Library Directors in a particular state.

To give you an example of a state that lists Librarians' contact information, I'll use Alabama, which is where I used to live and was the first state that I targeted for my Library marketing efforts. Upon Googling, "list of library directors in Alabama," the search yielded over twenty million results. I honed in on and reviewed the top three, which were:

- Directory of Public Libraries in Alabama
- Alabama Public Libraries
- Alabama Public Library Service

The Alabama Public Library Service had precisely the information I was seeking. On the site's landing page, next to the "Home" tab, there was a tab that read, "Public Library Listings." The listings had every Public Library in the state along with the Library's website address, if there was one, phone number, Director's name, and email address (see the following image). All I had to do was copy and paste each row into my "Database."

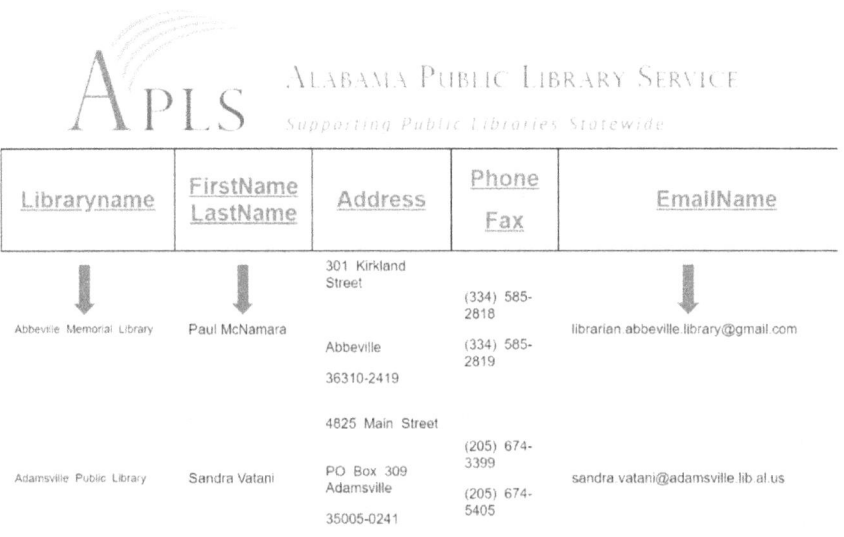

The State of North Carolina also had easily accessible information. When I searched for "State of North Carolina Libraries and Librarian contacts," one of the Google results was "Library Directory | State Library of North Carolina." Every Academic and Public Library in the State of North Carolina and its Head Librarian was listed, plus there was a downloadable spreadsheet to boot! Now, before you get overly excited, Alabama and North Carolina are more of an exception than the rule. For most of the Libraries in my "Database," I had to copy and paste the contact information manually from a Library's website. On average, I was able to add about twelve (12) Libraries an hour. Because of the time involved in loading the contacts, I decided to prioritize adding those states that had their Library contact information readily available in spreadsheet formats, first.

Another site that I found beneficial, and I believe you will too, is LibWeb (www.lib-web.org). The site contains information on State, Academic, Public, and other types of Libraries and Consortia that are in over one hundred forty-six (146) countries. One of the features of the website is, it allows you to click on a U.S. State, for instance, and be directed to Public Libraries within the State. Next, you can click on a Library's link, and be taken to its home page. Once you are on the Library's site, you can then search for key decision-makers who many times can be found in the "About Us," "Staff Directory," or similar section. While adding contacts manually from LibWeb will be more time consuming than having a spreadsheet with contacts already in it, the number of Libraries on the site is so robust; I wanted to make sure you were aware of the resource.

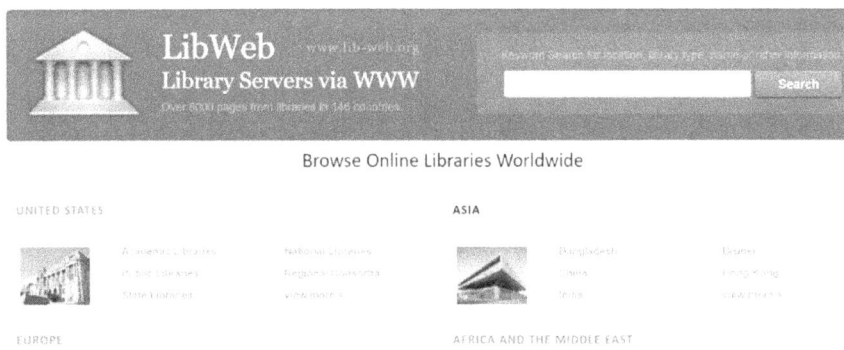

If you don't want to spend the time building a "Database" from scratch, I have two versions of my Library Contacts "Database" available for sale on my website, one with over three thousand (3000+) contacts and the other with five thousand (5000).

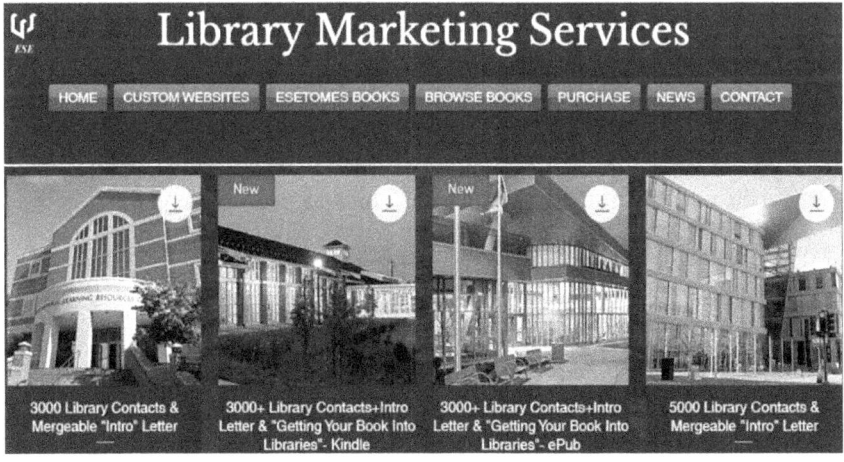

www.eseinc1.com/library-marketing-services

Chapter 8
Creating a "Mail Merge" Document

Now that you have your Libraries and Librarians in some type of "Database," if you want to use this data to correspond with more than one Librarian at a time, you can do so via a "Mail Merge." A "Mail Merge" allows you to create a batch of documents that are personalized for each recipient. To illustrate how this can be achieved, I'll refer to Microsoft Excel and Microsoft Word, but similar products should be able to deliver the same type of results.

Microsoft Word has a feature called "Step-by-Step Mail Merge Wizard," which allows you to insert data from an Excel spreadsheet into a Word document, thus giving the text a more "personalized" feel if you will. If you are unfamiliar with how to do a Word "Mail Merge," you can Google, "Mail merge using an Excel spreadsheet - Office Support," and Microsoft has instructions that will show you how. Your Google search will also reveal "how-to" videos as well.

With "Mail Merge," I can "customize" my "Marketing Campaign" letters to Libraries so that they don't have a "mass email" look. Here's how I go about it. I insert "merge fields" into several places in the document I plan to email so that it will look "tailored" to the individual. I can use any field heading in the "Database" to achieve this result. If my "Database" contains a heading of First_Name for the Librarian's first name, then my "merge field" in my Word document must be called First_Name as well. If I want to include the name of the Library in my letter, and the field heading in the "Database," is Library-Name, then I use Library-Name as the "merge field" in my correspondence. The more customized I want my document to look, the more headings I use from the "Database."

As a word of caution, before embarking on a massive email campaign to Librarians, be sure you look into the daily email limits of your provider. I learned the hard way that my Microsoft Outlook email subscription has a daily limit of 300 emails per day. I did a mailing of over 300 once and got locked out of my account. So do know what your daily limit is beforehand.

I use Excel's sort function in my Library Contacts "Database" to do "targeted" marketing campaigns. Let's say I want to email all of the Public Libraries in Ohio to make them aware there are currently sixteen Libraries in Ohio that have purchased my books. In the Public Libraries tab of the "Database," I do a sort by state and then add a new tab to the "Database" that I name, Ohio Mailing. Next, I copy and paste the field headings in the "Database" into the first row of the new Ohio Mailing tab. Third, I go back to the Public Libraries tab and cut and paste the Ohio Libraries into the new Ohio Mailing tab. In the body of my Word document, I will list the

Libraries in Ohio that have purchased one or more of my books and include "merge fields" that I think would be appropriate. Lastly, I use Word's "Step-by-Step Mail Merge Wizard" function, which will ask me the location of the data I want to use, which in this case will be the Ohio Libraries tab of my "Database," to send out my emails.

I try to be creative with my "messaging" in the Subject line of my Library emails. Using the Ohio Mailing example, I might put in the Subject line something like "ESETOMES Books in 16 Ohio Libraries" or "Not Far From The Tree" Popular With 16 Ohio Libraries." Mentioning Ohio and the quantification of the number of Libraries in the state that have my book are two **"hooks"** that I am using to try to create interest so that the recipient will open the email. Cognizant, you may not have any references or quantifiable data to share with a Library right now, your "hook" might be the connection between your book and an area of the Library's Collection Development Policy that it addresses. Or, you may have some other relevant information that you feel will get a Librarian's attention so that they will open your email.

Chapter 9
Tactics

To help better explain the tactics I'm using to get my books into Libraries, I put together a graphical depiction, which I believe captures the essence of what I'm doing. I tried to make the descriptions "catchy" so that they might be easier to retain. In a nutshell, my methodology is Research, Initiate, Review and Revise, Reinitiate, Repeat. I'll explain each.

- **Research** – do some homework before engaging a Library. For instance, you might learn from a Library's website that they belong to a consortium. You may decide to contact the consortium and all of its members with the thinking, if one member purchases, others are likely to follow

- **Initiate** – begin contacting Libraries

- **Review and Revise** – assess what happened when you made contact. Use what you have reviewed to modify what you previously did so that you can improve results. A good example here is, Google Analytics revealed Librarians were not clicking on the "Library References" link that I had started including in my emails, so, I went back to inputting my "Library References" list in my correspondence

- **Reinitiate** – implement your revisions

- **Repeat** – continue doing all of the above and keep refining even after you've had some success getting your book into Libraries

Eric's Library Tactics

Review and Revise

Initiate **Repeat** **Reinitiate**

Research

Tactics   Chapter 9

Email Content

Emails are my primary method for contacting Libraries. To date, ninety-seven percent (97%) of the Libraries that have purchased one or more of my books did so after receipt of, on average, 3.5 emails. If you are wondering why I don't make a lot of phone calls, well, back in January 2018, when I first started reaching out to Libraries, I sent emails and made phone calls. Invariably when I would call, I would be asked to send over my information, so I would end up having to send an email anyway. Also, there are just too many Libraries out there to try and call them one by one.

An Academic Librarian provided her perspective about emails in a comment to my *How To Get Your Book Into Libraries* article on TheCreativePenn site. She wrote, "If you really must e-mail a librarian directly, try approaching it like this, "my book relates to this area or class that I see is offered at your institution. The Librarian went on to say, "…if you have a moment, please take a look at my reviews (link) to see if this title would be a good fit for your collection" rather than outright requesting it be added to the collection." What jumped out at me in the comment was, "… my book relates to this area or class." That's the key for us self publishers, I believe! We have to be able to show Librarians the connection that exists between our books and their Libraries' needs as relates to books they feel their Patrons will want to read. When I think about it, my use of Library references in my emails is creating a connection between my books and ALA's Collection Development Policy criteria around, "Exhibit a high degree of potential user appeal and interest." By showing the list of Libraries that have purchased my books, I'm conveying, "My books have appeal, and they are generating interest."

The underlying construct of my emails to Libraries has remained virtually unchanged since 2018. I try to incorporate an attention-grabbing subject line, share "success" information about my books, including their sales performance, and I use an image such as my book(s) cover for visual effect. I also add an Amazon "Best Seller" screenshot, if I have one, provide Library references, share where my book(s) can be purchased, list their ISBNs, and place my Author's website beneath my signature line. While my emails may not include all of the above elements, I can pick and choose from the list.

If you don't have a Library reference, the other items above are still applicable, I feel. For sales information, I use my books' Amazon performance, which I keep track of in a spreadsheet. I get the data from "Author Central," which you will have access to once you load your book through KDP. Whenever my paperback sales go up, for instance, and the arrow has turned green in Author

Central, I note my ranking number, which in the case of paperbacks is out of over 8,000,000 books sold worldwide on Amazon.com, per Author Central's Best Seller ranking page. So let's say my Memoir reached a ranking of 109,306 today. It's worldwide ranking put it in the "Top 1.4" of all books sold worldwide on Amazon's site, if just for an hour. I use this positive development and might say in an email, "This month, *Not Far From The Tree*" peaked at being ranked in the "Top 1.4%" out of over 8,000,000 books sold worldwide on Amazon.com." Following is an example of how I show several months of sales performance in an email:

Recent ***Not Far From The Tree*** Amazon.com sales performance:

- October 9, 2019 "Top 1.4%" (number 109,306)
- September 19, 2019 "Top 1.5%" (number 118,589)
- August 3, 2019 "Top 1.6%" (number 126,922)
- July 14, 2019 "Top 1.2%" (number 95,722)

Should the Libraries I'm contacting have "book appeal" in their Collection Development Policies, which I believe most will, I'm addressing the requirement by providing factual and quantitative sales information from a known source (i.e., Amazon).

Tactics   Chapter 9

Which Libraries Should You Target First?

I suggest you target Libraries in the area in which you were born, the areas in which you currently and previously resided, and your local Public and Academic Libraries, first. The reason being is if you have written a quality piece of work, Libraries that you have a "geographic" connection with may be more inclined to consider your book and support you. I've found many Libraries to be supportive of "local" Authors and those with "geographic" ties. As an example, the Public Library in Little Rock, Arkansas, where I was born, purchased my Memoir after I made them aware, I was a "native son." Also, the Montgomery City-County Public Library purchased four copies of my Memoir, one copy of *#HTSP – How to Self-Publish* and three copies of *Getting Your Book Into Libraries* because of my former residential ties to the city. Once Libraries are aware of your local/geographic connection, you might get invited to speak about your book, which is what happened to me with my local Public Library.

When's the Best Time to Sell to Libraries?

Libraries tend to buy year-round, but by and large, I've found the briskest purchasing times to be during their Fiscal Year-End/Fiscal

Year-Begin (FYE/FYB) periods. It varies, but most of the Libraries I've contacted seem to have their FYE/FYB between April and July. In May 2019, the Institute of Museum and Library Services provided a listing of the Fiscal Years for Public Libraries, by state, for the year 2017. I would imagine the information is still pretty accurate.

Table 2. Reporting Periods of Public Libraries, by State: FY 2017

July 2016 through June 2017	January 2017 through December 2017	October 2016 through September 2017	Other[1]
Arizona	Arkansas	Alabama	Alaska[2]
California	Colorado	District of Columbia	Illinois[3]
Connecticut	Indiana	Florida	Maine[4]
Delaware	Kansas	Idaho	Michigan[5]
Georgia	Louisiana	Mississippi	Missouri[6]
Hawaii	Minnesota	American Samoa	Nebraska[7]
Iowa	New Jersey	Guam	New Hampshire[8]
Kentucky	North Dakota	Northern Marianas	New York[9]
Maryland	Ohio		Texas[10]
Massachusetts	Pennsylvania		Utah[8]
Montana	South Dakota		Vermont[7]
Nevada	Washington		
New Mexico	Wisconsin		
North Carolina			
Oklahoma			
Oregon			
Rhode Island			
South Carolina			
Tennessee			
Virginia			
West Virginia			
Wyoming			

[1] The reporting period varies among localities for the states in this column; however, each public library provided data for a 12-month period.
[2] January 2016 to June 2017.
[3] December 2015 to June 2017.
[4] April 2016 to December 2017.
[5] December 2015 to September 2017.
[6] January 2016 to October 2017.
[7] January 2016 to December 2017.
[8] July 2016 to December 2017.
[9] April 2016 to December 2017.
[10] February 2016 to December 2017.
SOURCE: IMLS, Public Libraries Survey, FY 2017.

Source: Institute of Museum and Library Services – "Public Libraries Survey Fiscal Year 2017" (Published May 2019)

Many of my Library sales have occurred when I've contacted Librarians the two months leading up to FYE, the month of FYB, and the month afterward. These timeframes are when they are, more than likely, spending both remaining and new funds.

Marketing Campaigns

I try to run a Library "Marketing Campaign" at least every two months, and when I do, I rotate through my Library Contacts "Database." The only times I contact all of the Libraries in the "Database" is when I have a significant price promotion, written a new book, or I have a new purchasing resource that I feel will be of interest to them. Otherwise, I'm doing "Targeted" campaigns where I'm focusing on, for example, a specific state like North Carolina where my "Introductory" email resulted in the purchase of five copies of *#HTSP - How to Self-Publish*, by a Public Library System.

In "The Science Behind Email Open Rates (and How to Get More People to Read Your Emails)," Steven MacDonald wrote, "… in 2019, the average email open rate dropped to 22.1%." While I'm not a big proponent of a lengthy email Subject line, I try to give enough information with a "hook," or two, to generate interest in opening the email, especially since, if MacDonald is correct, there's only a 22.1% chance the email will be opened. Some of the Subject line headings for my email marketing campaigns have been:

- ESETOMES eBooks Now Available Through Ingram

- ESETOMES eBooks and Paperbacks at 15% Off (COVID-19 Discount) thru June 5th

- "Not Far From The Tree" Baker & Taylor Availability

- Introducing "Getting Your Book Into Libraries"

Consider Using Multiple Email Addresses

If your email provider has a low daily rate for the number of emails you can send, you may need to consider using multiple email addresses to contact Libraries. I use three different addresses. Why? 1) To avoid the appearance of bombarding the email recipient, 2) If I want to send more than 300 emails at a time and 3) As a backup plan in case my email gets put into a "junk email" list. I'm not trying to be "sneaky" by using multiple email addresses. If emails are the best way for me to get information about my books in front of Librarians, and the most productive, I've got to find creative ways to do so because I believe my works merit their attention.

Purchase a Library Mailing List

For my "How To Get Your Book Into Libraries" article, I did some research to see if there were Library mailing lists that could be purchased and located one provided by Lists You Can Afford. At the time, the site listed Library contacts ranging from 900 to 23,000, with prices from $39 to $99. If you are looking for a vetted list that is generating proven results for a self publisher, however, a number of your peers have purchased and are using my Library Contacts "Database." It is available on my website, www.eseinc1.com/library-marketing-services, in 3,000 plus or 5,000 contact versions at affordable pricing, I feel. You get with the "Database," my "North Carolina Library Campaign" shell letter, so that you can get started contacting Libraries right away.

Chapter 10
Methodology Summary

To summarize my methodology or "secret sauce," if you will, in terms of the tactics I've been using to get my books into Libraries, they are:

- Bring to the table a well-written piece of work and try to find a connection between it and Libraries' Collection Development Policy

- Identify the primary decision-makers in a Library and sell "Top-Down," and "Bottom Up"

- Utilize a "Library Contacts Database"

- Incorporate Mail Merge so that "customized" emails can be sent

- Employ an image, use quantitative data, and provide references in correspondence when possible

- **Research, Initiate, Review and Revise, Reinitiate, Repeat**

Thank You!

My sincere thanks to you for purchasing the ***Self Publisher's Toolkit***. Please do share your thoughts about the book on your bookseller's website.

Here's wishing you the best of luck in self publishing and marketing your book to Libraries.

Respectfully,
Eric Otis Simmons

References

- ProQuest.com – "Self Publishing Grew 40 Percent in 2018, New Report Reveals" (October 15, 2019)
- Forbes.com - "While $26 Billion Publishing Industry Is Flat, This Vertical Segment Is Exploding. Leverage These Insights To Ride The Wave" by Bernhard Schroeder (October 30, 2019)
- Statista.com – "Number of writers and authors in the U.S. 2011-2019" by Amy Watson, (April 24, 2020)
- U.S. Census Bureau – U.S. 2019 Population Estimates
- InDesignSkills - "Best Fonts for Books: The Only 5 Fonts You'll Ever Need" http://www.indesignskills.com/inspiration/fonts-for-books/#
- Fiver.com - https://www.fiverr.com
- Owler.com – Fiverr's Top 10 Competitors (https://www.owler.com/company/fiverr)
- Entreprenuer.com - Definition of Packaging https://www.entrepreneur.com/encyclopedia/packaging
- Wikipedia – Definition of Writer's Block, List of writing genres https://en.wikipedia.org/wiki/List_of_writing_genres, Definition of RSS Feed
- Oxford Dictionary - Definition of Title
- Merriam-Webster - definition of genre
- SEG Wiki - Definition of ISBN
- Query*Tracker* – "Top 10 Genres" https://querytracker.net/top-10-genres.php
- The Richest.com - **"Which 5 Book Genres Make The Most Money?"** by Thomas Stewart (January 31, 2014)

References

- Nathan Bransford, "Book publishing glossary" https://blog.nathanbransford.com/book-publishing-glossary
- Bookjobs.com "Commonly Used Terms" - http://www.bookjobs.com/commonly-used-terms
- Joanna Penn – "Pros And Cons Of Traditional Publishing vs Self Publishing" https://www.thecreativepenn.com/self-publishing-vs-traditional/
- WrittenWordMedia.com – "The Top Ten Publishing Industry Trends Every Author Needs to Know in 2020" by Clayton Noblit (January 9, 2020) https://www.writtenwordmedia.com/the-top-ten-2020-publishing-industry-trends-every-author-needs-to-know
- Reedsy.com – "The 12 BEST Self-Publishing Companies of 2020" (April 22, 2019) https://blog.reedsy.com/best-self-publishing-companies
- Alliance of Independent Authors (ALLi) - "The Best Self-Publishing Services–and the Worst–Rated" https://selfpublishingadvice.org/best-self-publishing-services
- Smashwords.com – About https://www.smashwords.com/about
- Good e-Reader – "Draft2Digital is the Best Ebook Distribution Platform for Indie Authors" by Michael Kozlowski (August 1, 2017) https://goodereader.com/blog/e-book-news/draft2digital-is-the-best-ebook-distribution-platform-for-indie-authors
- KindlePreneur.com – "SMASHWORDS VS DRAFT2DIGITAL VS PUBLISHDRIVE REVIEW" by Dave Chesson https://kindlepreneur.com/smashwords-vs-draft2digital/
- Entrepreneur.com – "5 Things This Self-Published Author Did to Sell Over 20,000 Books With Almost No Money"

References

https://www.entrepreneur.com/article/279385

- eBook.com - Amazon's share of the eBook market is 67% https://about.ebooks.com/ebook-industry-news-feed/
- The Basics of Book Metadata and Keywords - IngramSpark https://www.ingramspark.com/blog/the-basics-of-book-metadata-and-keywords
- SelfPublishing.com – "KDP Rocket Review: 4 Ways to Use Publisher Rocket & If It's Worth It" by Nicholas Rossis (October 31, 2019)
  https://selfpublishing.com/kdp-rocket/#:~:text=KDP%20Rocket%2C%20now%20known%20as,self%2Dpublished%20and%20independent%20authors.&text=In%20today's%20booming%20self%2Dpublishing,sprouting%20up%20at%20record%20pace
- ebooklaunch.com – "Similarities and Differences Between Print Books and Ebooks" https://ebooklaunch.com/what-are-the-differences-between-a-print-book-and-an-ebook-with-re-flowable-text/#:~:text=The%20single%20most%20important%20difference,formatted%20with%20re%2Dflowable%20text.
- Google Copyright Infringement – https://www.google.com/webmasters/tools/dmca-notice?pli=1
- American Library Association – "Frequently Asked Questions from Authors and Publishers" http://www.ala.org/tools/topics/authorfaq
- Publication 525 (2019), Taxable and Nontaxable Income (Rev. February 2020) https://www.irs.gov/publications/p525#en_US_2019_publink1000229288

References

- KDP – Tax Forms https://kdp.amazon.com/en_US/help/topic/G201990460#no_form
- G2.com – "dlvr.it Alternatives & Competitors" https://www.g2.com/products/dlvr-it/competitors/alternatives
- 3D Issue – "What are the Differences Between .epub and .mobi?" https://www.3dissue.com/what-are-the-differences-between-epub-and-mobi/
- New Orleans Public Library website (http://www.nolalibrary.org/)
- Wikipedia
- IngramSpark.com – "How Indie Authors Can Get Their Books Into Libraries" by Robin Cutler and "The Importance of Reviews" (August 11, 2016) https://www.ingramspark.com/blog/how-indie-authors-can-get-their-books-into-libraries
- The International Federation of Library Associations and Institutions (IFLA) – "Library Map of The World" (downloaded on June 19, 2020)
- Pew Research Center – "Most Americans – especially Millennials – say libraries can help them find reliable, trustworthy information" by A.W. Geiger (August 30, 2017)
- ReedsyBlog – "5 Reasons Why Selling to Libraries Needs to be a Top Priority" by Amy Collins (February 22, 2017)
- KirkusReviews.com
- TheCreativePenn.com – "How To Get Your Book Into Libraries" by Eric Otis Simmons (https://www.thecreativepenn.com/2019/06/12/book-marketing-how-to-get-your-book-into-libraries/)

References

- BookLife.com
- American Library Association – "Selection Criteria" http://www.ala.org/tools/challengesupport/selectionpolicytoolkit/criteria
- AmericanLibrariesMagazine.org - "OverDrive's New Owners: What It Means" by Marshall Breeding (December 31, 2019) https://americanlibrariesmagazine.org/blogs/the-scoop/overdrives-new-owners-what-means
- Draft2Digital – "What are your library payment options?" https://www.draft2digital.com/library-pricing
- Baker & Taylor - https://www.baker-taylor.com
- LibWeb.com
- Institute of Museum and Library Services – "Public Libraries Survey Fiscal Year 2017" (Published May 2019)
- SuperOffice.com - "The Science Behind Email Open Rates (and How to Get More People to Read Your Emails)" by Steven MacDonald https://www.superoffice.com/blog/email-open-rates/
- Fulton County Library System website (http://afpls.org/)

www.ingramcontent.com/pod-product-compliance
Lightning Source LLC
Chambersburg PA
CBHW071405290426
44108CB00014B/1694